2|7|1

WENDY &

CW00349313

ASSEMBLIES

With optional follow-up work for the class-room

ANTHONY GREENSLADE
and
HERBERT COOKE

Published by:
National Christian Education Council
Robert Denholm House
Nutfield
Redhill
RH1 4HW

ISBN 0-7197-0387-5

First published 1984
© 1983 Anthony Greenslade and Herbert Cooke

Typeset by Avonset, Midsomer Norton, Bath
Printed in Great Britain by BPCC Wheatons Ltd, Exeter

Contents

Introduction

Assemblies for 8-12s provides all the material needed for the Assemblies suggested. It includes talks, stories, Bible readings with comments, poems, prayers and suggestions for appropriate hymns.

Suggestions for follow-up work for the class-room are also included. These provide material for teachers to use the stimulus given by an Assembly in their general religious education work.

Some of the hymns and songs suggested are well known and may be found in standard hymn books. Less well-known songs have been selected from two books in common use in Middle Schools: *Come and Praise* (BBC) and *Sing New Songs* (NCEC).

Most of the Bible readings reproduced in full are from the *Good News Bible.* A list of these passages will be found at the end of the book.

A new school year

The Assembly

Introduction
Invite the children to put up their hands if they collect coins. Ask what a coin collector is called. (Numismatist) Coins are graded according to their condition. The very best grade is called F D C which stands for *fleur de coin*. A coin graded F D C is quite perfect with no marks. Of course, very few coins are F D C grade. There is just a chance that an old coin was put away before it was circulated and then found many years, perhaps centuries, later. Such coins are like new: we say they are in mint condition. But most coins go into use: that is why they are made. They get rubbed against others. They are dropped. They are put into machines. Sometimes they get so worn that it is hard to tell what they are. Ask if anyone has an old Victorian penny like that.

Hymn
New every morning is the love

Talk
We are rather like coins. We start out in mint condition and end up all marked and worn. But every so often we get the chance to begin afresh. In a way every day is like that, as John Keble, the writer of the hymn we have just sung, said. God's love comes to us fresh and new every morning. Some people make a fresh start on New Year's Day. They make resolutions, promises to try to be better people. You may have done that.

We have a chance to make a fresh start today because this is the beginning of a new school year. It is F D C in mint condition. It has no marks. It is new for everyone: for all the staff in the kitchen, for the cleaning staff, for the teachers and for all of you. Let us do what we can to make it a good year, so that its marks, and there are sure to be some, are honourable ones. Here is one way we can help.

For some children this is a specially important new school year: for the new boys and girls. When you were new you probably felt rather small and very strange. You may have thought some of the older pupils looked rather frightening. And as for the teachers! All of you who have been here a while can start the year well by being kind and helpful to those who feel very new and strange. And all you new boys and girls will very soon feel quite at home.

Everyone gets a new start in a new year. We have all made mistakes in the past. Wise people learn from their mistakes.

Poem/Prayer
This poem about the New Year was written for 1 January, but it applies just as well to us today.

The New Year

Father, we like things that are new.
A new white sheet of paper on which to write or draw,
A new shirt or tie, a new skirt or dress,
A new bike, a new car,
A new crusty loaf,
A new game, a new style,
A new tune, a new scene,
A new book, a new friend,
A new opportunity for fun and service.

Thank you, Father, for this New Year,
For a new chance to begin again.
It stretches before us unused.
You say to us,
'Put behind you what is past.
Your disappointments. Your failures.
Your lost opportunities.
Begin from here.
I make all things new.'

Thank you, Father,
We will look forward, not back,
We will fix our eyes upon the living Christ,
Whom we know as Jesus of Nazareth.

We will walk through the year with him.
By his help, in his strength,
We will overcome.

(Jack and Edna Young)

Bible reading
During the last supper which Jesus shared with his disciples, he said to them:

'And now I give you a new commandment: love one another. As I have loved you, so you must love one another. If you have love for one another, then everyone will know that you are my disciples.'

(John 13.34-35, GNB)

Hymns
Growing, growing   (SNS 62)
Life is like a journey   (SNS 67)
Lord of all hopefulness   (CP 52)
Morning has broken   (CP 1)

Prayer
Help us, heavenly Father, in this new year to work hard and to play hard. May we put behind us the mistakes we made last year. May we resolve in our hearts to be more thoughtful, and kind to each other. We cannot all be very clever or very strong, but we can all remember Jesus' new commandment, to love one another.

The Lord's Prayer

Follow-up for the class-room

1   Make a list of all the occasions in the year when a new start can be made. Choose one and write about it.

2   New things have a special kind of beauty. Look at a new book. Why does it have a special kind of feel? Smell it. Think about other new things: a puppy, a sheet of paper, a bulb or shoot. Write a poem about one of them.

3   Jesus told two very short parables about the newness of his work. Read Luke 5.36-39. In one sense Jesus was building on the foundations of the Jewish faith; but in another sense his gospel was quite unlike anything that had gone before. Discuss in what ways Jesus' work was different, so different that his disciples said he was the Son of God. The following references will be useful: Mark 1.22; Matthew 16.13-16; Matthew 21.33-40.

Friendship

The Assembly

Preparation
Ask a group of children to write a short paragraph each on the subject *A friend is* . . . Choose several to be read at the assembly.

Introduction
Invite the children to tell you the difference between an acquaintance and a friend. (We have many acquaintances, people we know up to a point. Friends are special. We do not have so many and we know them very well.)

Read, or ask the children to read, some of the paragraphs on *A friend is* . . . The selection made should bring out ideas such as: We like to be with friends. We feel a sense of loss when they are not there. We feel comfortable with friends. We do not need to talk a lot. We can be ourselves with them; we do not have to pretend. Friends make us feel safe and happy. We stick up for them. There is a bond of loyalty. We share things. We will put ourselves out for them. We fall out at times but we are quick to make up our quarrels. We give and take. We understand each other.

Story: Two famous friends
David and Jonathan had become close friends. Although David was only a shepherd and Jonathan was a prince—King Saul's son—they had liked each other from the moment they met. They made a solemn promise to each other that they would always remain friends.

Later, David became an officer in the army of Israel. He was a very successful leader of his soldiers and he fast became a popular hero. When he came back from forays against the Philistines the crowds welcomed him with great shouting and cheering. 'Saul has killed thousands,' they cried, 'but David has killed tens of thousands.' Saul did not like this: kings do not like to be reminded that some young officer is a better leader than they are! Saul became jealous of David. He became very angry. Already Saul was suffering from a mental illness which made him quite unpredictable. He could fly into a ferocious rage for no real reason. His whole fury became directed against David, and Saul plotted to kill him.

Once, when David was playing his harp in Saul's house, Saul threw his spear at him. Had David not been quick on his feet he would have been killed then. Another time, only quick thinking by Michal, David's wife, saved him when Saul sent soldiers to David's house. It seemed clear that David would have to run away to save his life. First he would see his friend Jonathan again and give King Saul one more chance to take him back. David was loyal to Saul and would do nothing to hurt him.

David and Jonathan met secretly. Jonathan was very sad when he learned why David wished to go away. It was not easy for the king's son to believe that his father really wanted to kill David. However he agreed to test Saul. There was to be a great feast extending over several days to mark the new moon. David's place would be empty and without doubt the king would notice it. Jonathan would tell his father that David had been called home to Bethlehem for a special family feast and had asked permission to go. If Saul seemed to accept the excuse calmly all would be well. But if he fell into a rage and threatened David, then Jonathan would warn him.

They arranged a special meeting place in a field they both knew with some low rocks which made a good hiding place. They arranged a secret signal: Jonathan would fire three arrows at the rocks behind which David hid. If he shouted to his servant who was picking up the arrows, 'The arrows are on this side of you, get them', all would be well. But if he shouted, 'The arrows are on the other side of you', then David would know that he had to leave quickly.

Jonathan did as he had agreed with his friend. On the first night Saul noticed David's absence but said nothing. The next night he asked his son why David was not in his place. Jonathan gave the excuse they had arranged. Saul began to curse and swear at Jonathan. He accused him of taking David's side against him. He warned Jonathan that although *he* should be the next king in Israel, he never would be while David lived. 'Bring him here; he must die,' raved Saul. But Jonathan refused to be swayed despite all Saul could say. 'Why should he die? What has he done?' demanded Jonathan.

Then Saul in an insane anger seized his spear and threw it viciously at his own son to kill him. Fortunately he missed. Jonathan now knew that David would never be safe while Saul lived. He was bitterly angry with his father. Next morning he went with a servant boy to the meeting place and fired off his arrows. The boy ran to pick them up. 'The arrow is further on,' shouted Jonathan. 'Get a move on, hurry!' David heard and knew that he must flee for his life.

(Story based on part of 1 Samuel 18—20)

Why do you think that David and Jonathan's friendship has become a sort of pattern for what true friendship should be? (The two friends trusted each other without question.) Jonathan's loyalty put him into great danger. Even though he knew there was truth in Saul's jibe that David would be the next king if he lived, Jonathan did not let this sway him. Incidentally, both David and Jonathan remained loyal to King Saul although it was far from easy.

Reading
Jesus liked having close friends, just as we do. They lived together and shared many hardships. His friends had given up everything to be with Jesus. But Jesus knew that there were dangers even in friendship. He said:

'If you love only the people who love you, why should you receive a blessing? Even sinners love those who love them! And if you do good only to those who do good to you, why should you receive a blessing? Even sinners do that! And if you lend only to those from whom you hope to get it back, why should you receive a blessing? Even sinners lend to sinners, to get back the same amount! No! Love your enemies and do good to them; lend and expect nothing back. You will then have a great reward, and you will be sons of the Most High God. For he is good to the ungrateful and the wicked. Be merciful just as your Father is merciful.'

(Luke 6.32-36, GNB)

That's surprising! Friendship can keep others out. People can be so happy in their friendships that they forget others. It is easy to be friendly and loving with those we like and who like us. Jesus calls us to spread our friendship much wider. Friendship is great. It is such a good thing that we must learn to spread it all round us. It is not easy, but then Jesus never said it would be!

Hymns
Heavenly Father, may thy blessing   (CP 62)
If you have a friend, man   (SNS 82)
I will bring to you the best gift I can offer   (CP 59)
  (especially verse 3)

Prayer
Heavenly Father, it is grand to have friends. Help us to make our friendships grow by understanding what loyalty means and by being prepared to share and to forgive.

  We pray that our friendships may never make others feel left out, unwanted or sad. May we be on the lookout for ways to offer friendship to those who need it. We remember that Jesus offers us his friendship; help us to respond by showing friendship to others.

Follow-up for the class-room

1   Jesus called different kinds of people to be his disciples. Read Mark 1.14-20. Who were these men and what was their job? Discuss what seems surprising in Jesus' choice. Read Luke 5.27-32. Why might it have been difficult for Levi to follow Jesus? Read John 1.43-45. Here Jesus calls two more of his disciples; what are their names? Complete the list of disciples by reading Mark 3.16-18.

2   Arrange and carry out a project to show friendship to someone who is ill or in special need, eg, send harvest gifts with letters to someone in hospital; or if there is a current appeal, such as is made from time to time on *Blue Peter*, do something to help.

3   Introduce the following problem to the group: Imagine that you try to be friendly with a boy or girl who seems to be very lonely, and you are rejected. Should you persist? Write about what you would do.

Being human — 1: People can choose

The Assembly

Preparation
Either obtain a cassette tape that has computer programmes on it (most small home computers use cassette tape back-up) together with an ordinary cassette player; *or* have blackboard and chalk, or poster paper and thick felt pens, ready for use.

Introduction
Either Play the computer tape on an ordinary cassette player. Two notes only will be heard. The notes vary in length, and give information in code form that the computer understands. The computer can only act on the information given to it.

Or A computer does not understand the letter A. When a letter A is pressed on a computer keyboard, the machine turns it into a code. This code can be represented by 1's and 0's, or by high and low notes, or by greens and reds. Inside the computer the code is in tiny electrical pulses. On a board write up examples:

A=00100001   _⎍_⎍___⎍_   RRGRRRRG

Z=00111010   _⎍‾‾⎍⎍_   RRGGGRGR

Because computers can process very, very quickly the information codes they are given, they are an important part of our lives.

Whichever introduction is used, go on to ask the children to give as many examples of the use of computers as they can think of, eg, for calculations; translating languages; playing games; diagnosing illnesses; storing information such as car registrations, descriptions of people for police work; designing machines and buildings; playing tunes; stock control in large firms, etc.

Story

Computers play a big part in our lives. Already there are factories which produce cars from design to finished product with every stage computer-controlled. Nearly all our regular bills for gas, electricity, telephone and so on are calculated by computers.

Like most of us, Mr Brown did not enjoy getting bills, especially gas bills. They seemed to grow bigger every quarter. So, when the latest gas bill landed on the mat, he was not too eager to open it. When he did pluck up courage he had an even bigger shock than he expected. Amount due, announced the bill, £10,999.99. With shaking hand Mr Brown reached for the phone and rang the accounts department.

The young lady who answered was polite and helpful. 'Oh dear,' she said soothingly, 'that does seem rather a lot even for the heavy quarter. Leave it with me and I'll ring back.'

Mr Brown sat biting his nails until the phone rang. 'Yes, Mr Brown,' said the same soothing voice, 'I'm afraid it's the computer's fault. We'll send you another account.'

Mr Brown was so relieved that he did not question the polite young lady. But there was something wrong about her explanation of what had happened. What do you think it was?

Of course, computers cannot be blamed because they cannot really make mistakes or tell lies. They can blow a fuse, or break down, but they cannot, provided they are given the correct information, make mistakes. What usually happens is that they are wrongly programmed. Some *person* has made a mistake, not the computer. All the information a computer has in its memory banks is put there by someone. It cannot choose what to do; it can only do what it is programmed to do.

People can choose: they can choose to do or not to do things. They can do things which are right, or which they know are wrong.

Readings

When Jesus called people to follow him they had to make up their own minds: they had to choose. In the first reading those who were called, chose to go; in the second reading the young man chose not to. As you listen to it, try to decide why he made that choice.

As Jesus walked along the shore of Lake Galilee, he saw two fishermen, Simon and his brother Andrew, catching fish with a net. Jesus said to them, 'Come with me, and I will teach you to catch men.' At

14

once they left their nets and went with him.

He went a little farther on and saw two other brothers, James and John, the sons of Zebedee. They were in their boat getting their nets ready. As soon as Jesus saw them, he called them; they left their father Zebedee in the boat with the hired men and went with Jesus.

(Mark 1.16-20, GNB)

Once a man came to Jesus. 'Teacher,' he asked, 'what good thing must I do to receive eternal life?'

'Why do you ask me concerning what is good?' answered Jesus. 'There is only One who is good. Keep the commandments if you want to enter life.'

'What commandments?' he asked.

Jesus answered, 'Do not commit murder; do not commit adultery; do not steal; do not accuse anyone falsely; respect your father and your mother; and love your neighbour as you love yourself.'

'I have obeyed all these commandments,' the young man replied. 'What else do I need to do?'

Jesus said to him, 'If you want to be perfect, go and sell all you have and given the money to the poor, and you will have riches in heaven; then come and follow me.'

When the young man heard this, he went away sad, because he was very rich.

(Matthew 19.16-22, GNB)

Each one of us has to make up his or her own mind that they want to follow Jesus. The choice is ours.

Hymns
I've heard of one called Jesus   (SNS 32)
The journey of life may be easy, may be hard   (CP 45)
When greedy people grab and take   (SNS 79)

Prayer
We thank you, God, that we have minds of our own, that we can choose. We are sorry for the times we have made wrong choices. We know that Jesus wants us to follow him, but he will not force us to follow. Help us as we learn more about him to make the right decision.

Follow-up for the class-room

1   Computers can be used to eliminate many boring, repetitive jobs; but can also cause unemployment. They can store very efficient medical or personal records; but this information can also be used in wrong ways to limit people's freedom. Is the invention and use of computers a good thing or a bad thing? Ask each child to write down what he/she thinks.

2   Each child makes a list of everyday situations in which a choice has to be made, eg, finding a coin or book in the playground. Alongside each situation, he writes the possible choices for action, and underlines the one which he thinks is the right choice, eg, handing in the coin or book.

3   The Bible has stories of many people who had to make choices. Look up each of these references and write down what choice had to be made: Luke 22.3-6; Luke 22.39-45; Luke 23.13-23.

4   Have a group discussion on the subject, 'Should you *always* tell the truth?'

Being human — 2: People are different

The Assembly

Preparation
If the alternative approach is being made during the Talk, arrange for the children to show their skills in appropriate ways. Choose a child to read the poem.

Story and talk
Some people hate others to be different from themselves. Even children sometimes make fun of someone because he or she is different in some way from themselves. This makes a great deal of trouble in the world.

Long, long ago in ancient Greece, there lived, near a place called Eleusis, a robber named Procrustes (which means the Stretcher). He was a cruel and wicked man who used to invite weary travellers to stay at his house. There he fed them well, plying them with wine to make them drowsy. After supper he overpowered them and fastened them securely on a special bed. If they were too short he stretched them until they fitted the bed. If they were too long he cut off their legs.

One of the travellers he invited to stay was the hero Theseus. Theseus was suspicious, and only pretended to drink the wine he was offered. He kept his wits about him, and when Procrustes seized him, Theseus overpowered the cruel robber. He killed Procrustes by fastening *him* to the bed, and as he was too long Theseus cut off *his* legs.

Now someone who tries to make everyone fit the same pattern is called Procrustean.

Procrustes was a horrible man. We all know that people *are* different, but many of us fail to *enjoy* the differences.

(Bring out a group or class to sit at the front facing the rest of the school.) Pick out some tall children and ask them to stand up. Then choose some small children; ask them to stand. If there are some with different coloured

17

skins, ask them to stand, explaining where their families originated. Point out that there is a good range of skin colour among so-called white people, too. Ask those with fair hair to stand, then those with dark hair. *(Continue until every child is standing up.)*

The features that have been mentioned show something of the mixture of races that make up natives of the United Kingdom. The great variety in appearance adds to the interest and enjoyment of life. *(Children return to places.)*

But more wonderful still, inside every cell in our bodies there is a kind of code which is different for every person in the world, except identical twins. This means that no two people are exactly alike, and even identical twins develop differently as they grow older. Not only are there different races, but every individual in every race is unique.

Either Ask the children to raise their hands to indicate things they are good at or keen on. Include school activities, such as reading, mathematics, football, running, rounders; home and hobbies activities, such as gardening, caring for pets, cooking, ice-skating, washing up. Comment on the wide range covered. We are different; we like different things; we have different abilities.

Or Show the results of the skills of some children *(see Preparation)*. One could show a piece of art, another a model; one could sing a solo or one of the verses of the hymn; another could play an instrument or read an original poem or story.

We should not be jealous because someone can do something better than we can. We can enjoy the pictures others paint, the music they make. We can delight in a garden someone has made lovely, enjoy a tasty meal someone has cooked. We all have different abilities and we can enjoy each other's skills.

Reading
Jesus said,

'For only a penny you can buy two sparrows, yet not one sparrow falls to the ground without your Father's consent. As for you, even the hairs of your head have all been counted. So do not be afraid; you are worth much more than many sparrows!'

(Matthew 10.29-31, GNB)

Comment

Jesus wanted people to understand that God loved each one of them. This is true for us too. God loves each of us as a unique person. For him no one is more important than another. No one gets more care or love than another.

Poem *(read by a child)*

Differences
Thousands of different leaves on a tree;
Millions of different waves on the sea;
Different animals, different birds;
Different voices, and different words;
Different stories, in different books;
Different people, with different looks;
I'm not like you, and you're not like me:
But we all belong to God's family.

(Lilian Cox)

Hymns

All over the world   (CP 61)
God is love   (CP 36)
This is the world that God has made   (SNS 8)
We all were born at different times   (SNS 59)
   (Change 'church' to 'school' in verse 3)

Prayer

We thank you, Father, that there are so many different kinds of people in the world. Thank you for the gifts you have given to each of us. Help us to use our gifts and develop them so that we can help and delight others.

   We thank you that we can enjoy the gifts of others. May we never be jealous, but rather delight in the work of many hands and minds.

Music

Close with a record by a solo instrumentalist, eg, James Galway.

Follow-up for the class-room

1   Many differences are apparent in nature. Read about snowflakes and how they are formed. Invent some snowflake patterns by folding a piece of paper as in the diagram and cutting out shapes along each folded side.

2   Discuss why an orchestra sounds so rich. Find out about the different sections and write a sentence or two about each.

3   For older children: Find out about chromosomes and genes.

4   In pairs draw a portrait of each other. Mount the results to make a picture gallery. Comment on the variety. Let the children imagine a place where everyone looked alike, liked and disliked the same things, and had the same abilities. Would they like to live in such a place? Discuss; or write down the reasons for the answers.

5   One of the things that seems to make people appear different is that they have different religious beliefs. Find out about one other religion, noting similarities as well as differences.

Being human — 3: Things we need

The Assembly

Preparation
You will need a large sheet of paper and felt pen, or a blackboard and chalk. In the centre either draw or fix an illustration of a boy and girl about ten years of age. As the assembly progresses fill in the needs discovered, as in the diagram below.

Introduction
Here is a picture of a boy and girl about the same age as some of you. We are going to think about some of the things they need in order to live and develop into healthy, happy men and women.

Talk
What are the essential things all living creatures need to keep them alive? Most important of all is liquid of some kind. Without water we would die within a few days. We could last longer without food. But after a few weeks we would become very ill and die.

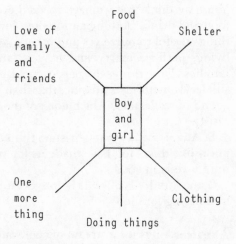

Now think about cold days and nights, rain and wind, snow and frost. We need the protection provided by clothing and shelter. Even in Britain without this protection we could very soon die of exposure. We sometimes hear of cases where unwary hikers have died of exposure on a moor or in the hills, sometimes almost within calling distance of a cottage.

If we are well fed, and protected from the weather, with good clothes and a warm, comfortable home, would we always be happy? We could be very unhappy even then. What else do we need? We need people to love and care for us. When we are tiny babies, parents give us all the love we need. Baby is happy when he is cuddled and played with. But we need to feel wanted and loved right through life. That is why family and friends are so important. It is equally important for us to be able to show love and care for others.

Is that enough to satisfy us? What about those times when we see other people doing well, perhaps at lessons, making things, playing games, doing things so much better than we can do them? We all need to feel we can do things, too. Everyone needs to feel that they can achieve something, that they can give things to the people around them. Of course we cannot be good at everything but we must feel we can do something. It is very important for everyone, and that includes young and old, clever and not so clever, strong of body and those who are handicapped.

You may think that we have covered every possible need now. We have food and drink, clothing and shelter, love and friendship, and we can do things useful to ourselves and others. When we grow up we can earn a living, perhaps marry and have a family of our own, and give our families all the things they need, too. But many people who have all that still feel something is missing, that their lives are not complete. They feel a kind of restlessness which none of the things we have talked about can satisfy.

St Augustine, a great Christian thinker who lived many centuries ago, put it like this: 'You have made us for yourself, and our heart is restless until it rests in you.'

Some hundreds of years before St Augustine, a Hebrew poet wrote of his longing for God:

As a deer longs for a stream of cool water,
    so I long for you, O God.

I thirst for you, the living God;
    when can I go and worship in your presence?

(Psalm 42.1-2, GNB)

Christians believe that God has made us in such a way that we can only be fully happy when we come to know him. Knowing God is something that is important not only for this life, but for ever. That is why living without God leaves us feeling as though something of the greatest importance is missing.

Hymns
I grasp at the air   (SNS 63)
The Lord's my shepherd, I'll not want

Prayer
We thank you, God, for all the good things we enjoy: for food and warmth, for homes in which we find love and care. We thank you for our skills: that we are able to make things with our hands, that we can read what others have written, that we can write stories of our own. We pray that we may learn to know and love you, our heavenly Father, and so find true happiness.

Follow-up for the class-room

1   Make a poster similar to the rough one built up at assembly. Ask different children to produce paintings illustrating the various needs discussed, eg,
Food such as fruits, vegetables, cereals, etc;
Shelter, different kinds of houses, and clothing;
Human love, families and friends;
Achievements, reading, writing, arts and crafts, skills of all kinds;
Knowing God, praying, reading the Bible, singing hymns.
    Arrange a selection of the pictures round the central diagram of a boy and a girl.

2   Read Matthew 10.29-31. These few verses give us some idea of the love that God has for each one of us.

3   Children at the top end of the age range could read George Herbert's poem *The Pulley*. The ideas it expresses are those emphasised in the assembly. The language is basically simple, but some words need explanation:
Stanza 1, line 4—dispersèd: spread out
Stanza 2, line 3—God made a stay: God stopped what he was doing
Stanza 4, line 2—repining: being discontented.

The Pulley
        When God at first made man,
Having a glass of blessings standing by,
'Let us,' said he, 'pour on him all we can;
Let the world's riches, which dispersèd lie,
                Contract into a span.'

        So strength first made a way;
Then beauty flowed, then wisdom, honour, pleasure;
When almost all was out, God made a stay,
Perceiving that, alone of all his treasure,
                Rest in the bottom lay.

        'For if I should', said he,
'Bestow this jewel also on my creature,
He would adore my gifts instead of me,
and rest in Nature, not the God of Nature:
                So both should losers be.

        'Yet let him keep the rest,
But keep them with repining restlessness;
Let him be rich and weary, that at least,
If goodness lead him not, yet weariness
                May toss him to my breast.'

Harvest time

The Assembly

Preparation
If you are not having a full harvest display, arrange for a token harvest, to include flowers, fruits, vegetables, an object made of wood and one of metal. Also include a modern artefact such as a vacuum cleaner. Arrange for the group-reading from Deuteronomy.

Introduction
When something has been manufactured, such as this vacuum cleaner, we sometimes forget that the raw materials from which it is made come from the earth. Invite the children to tell you what materials were used. As each is mentioned, give its derivative. (The metal parts come from metal ores such as iron which have to be dug out of the ground. The plastic parts come from oil which also comes out of the ground. The rubber parts come from a tree.) These are a kind of harvest, too.

Nowadays we have our harvest thanksgiving at the end of September or the beginning of October. This is when the harvest of the fields has been gathered in and we thank God for giving us the fruits of the earth.

Long ago there was a harvest called Lammas. It goes back well over a thousand years. Some people think it began in the time of King Alfred the Great. We know that Alfred was very interested in the church and its worship. The word Lammas comes from two Anglo-Saxon words: *hlaf* (a loaf) and *maesse* (a feast). In time this became *Llammaesse* which was later simplified to Lammas.

Anglo-Saxon is sometimes called Old English. It was the language spoken by the people of our land before the Norman conquest. Lammas was fixed on 1 August. Why does 1 August seem a strange time to have a harvest festival? (Only the first part of the harvest is ready to be gathered by then.) Some years there would be very little grain ready to be harvested. The first ears of corn were taken and the grains were ground into flour to make a loaf. This loaf was put on the altar in the church and was used for the communion. So Lammas is a feast of first-fruits. It is a loaf-mass.

At Lammas time the people thanked God for blessing them with the first-fruits, and also prayed that the rest of the harvest would be good, to carry them through the long, dark months of winter. Even today harvest time can be an anxious time for farmers. Why is this?

Reading

Long ago in Judaea, hundreds of years before Jesus lived, the Jews remembered at harvest time those who were poor: people who had no land of their own, foreigners, children who had lost their parents, women whose husbands had died. We can read about this in one of the Jewish Law books called Deuteronomy.

Group 1: When you gather your crops and fail to bring in some of the corn that you have cut, do not go back for it; it is to be left for the foreigners, orphans, and widows, so that the Lord your God will bless you in everything you do.
Group 2: When you have picked your olives once, do not go back and get those that are left; they are for the foreigners, orphans, and widows.
Group 3: When you have gathered your grapes once, do not go back over the vines a second time; the grapes that are left are for the foreigners, orphans and widows.
All: Never forget that you were slaves in Egypt; that is why I have given you this command.

(Deuteronomy 24.19-22, GNB)

Helping today

If the school normally has a collection for Christian Aid, Oxfam, or some similar organisation, display pictures of their work. The two main ways in which these organisations try to help countries in the Third World are:
1   To relieve immediate distress;
2   To help people to help themselves by providing water, simple machinery and knowledge.

Hymns

Father of all the peoples   (SNS 53)
Fill your hearts with joy and gladness   (CP 9)
Praise God, all living things   (SNS 7)
When the poor man asks for money   (SNS 81)

Prayer

We come today, heavenly Father, to thank you for your good gifts and for those who work hard to provide us with food. Thank you for the rich minerals of the earth: coal, metal ores, and minerals, from which so much is made for our comfort and enjoyment. Thank you for the trees which provide us with wood for our homes and furniture; and paper to make the books we read. Thank you for plants and flowers which give us pleasure by their beauty and scent.

Amidst all the plenty of our harvest, may we not forget those who have little to eat, those who need our careful thought so that the help we give will enable them to grow and develop their own lands.

Follow-up for the class-room

1   Make a careful drawing of a cut apple, tomato or pepper, etc.

2   Find out how people of other faiths celebrate harvest, eg, the Jewish Sukkot Festival.

3   Arrange to take gifts of fruit, etc, to some sick or elderly people who live near your school. Design and make cards to go with the gifts.

4   Make a display of packets, wrappers and (empty) tins which contained food from other lands. Find out the countries of origin, and how the food is grown and packaged.

5   Make a list of reasons why people in the Third World need help in providing their own food, and discuss ways in which they can be helped.

Good out of evil—Remembrance

The Assembly

Preparation
If you have Remembrance Day poppies in the school, use this Assembly after they have been distributed.

A large picture of the Coventry Cathedral cross made from charred timbers, and a picture or model of the cross of nails will be needed. (CEM publishes a pack of *Easter Pictures* which contains a suitable picture.)

Have a Red Cross flag ready to show.

Introduction
Ask the children why poppies are sold during the few days prior to 11 November each year. (To show our remembrance of those who lost their lives in war.) None of us can remember the First World War, 1914-1918. A few may remember the Second World War, 1939-1945. But everyone knows that soldiers lose their lives in Northern Ireland and in 1982 some soldiers, sailors, airmen and civilians were killed in the Falkland Islands. War is a terrible and evil thing. It may be exciting to watch war films in the comfort of our living rooms; but in war, many die terrible deaths, others are hideously wounded and suffer for the rest of their lives. It is not only soldiers who suffer, but also ordinary men, women and children. People lose their homes and those they love. In a recent war in the Lebanon an old man was interviewed after a bombing raid by Israeli planes. He lost his wife, his daughter, and his four grandchildren in that raid; he had no home left, either, but that was the least of his worries at that time.

But, terrible though war is, good can come out of it. Here is a story of how one man's experience led to the setting-up of a great international organisation.

Story: The Red Cross

Henri Dunant was a rich young Swiss banker. In June 1859 he was on a tour of northern Italy when he found himself caught up in a war. The French and Sardinians under Emperor Napoleon III of France were fighting against the Austrians. The battle centred on a village called Solferino. The armies involved were quite large, over 100,000 men on each side. At that time weapons were quite deadly: guns and cannon were used. Particularly deadly were the grenades—hollow bombs filled with metal fragments—which could cause terrible flesh wounds.

Henri Dunant was horrified by what he saw that day. It was bad enough to see the dead lying in grotesque attitudes all around, but the living wounded were far worse. The French had been ordered to attack Solferino itself, which stood on a hill. The defending artillery had caused havoc, slaughtering and wounding thousands of attacking Frenchmen, before the village fell. Wounded men were everywhere, crying out for help. Some had lost arms and legs. Many were bleeding from terrible wounds. But no help came. Comrades helped each other as best they could, but the badly wounded were left to die. Dunant did what he could. He pleaded with the villagers to take the wounded into their homes. Soon all the cottages were filled with injured soldiers, but many died because there was no proper medical help.

Dunant determined to do something about this terrible situation. He wrote a book called *A Souvenir of Solferino*. He described what he had seen and the shocking way in which soldiers were left to die without help. He pleaded for countries to organise volunteers into detachments to serve the wounded. In 1863 there was an international convention in Geneva at which sixteen countries were represented. A year later the Geneva Convention was signed. The countries agreed that each nation should have a voluntary aid society for war casualties which would be recognised by all governments. The aid society would give impartial medical attention to the wounded of both sides in war.

At last something was being done to help the wounded, the prisoners and others who suffered in war. Henri Dunant chose as the symbol of the new organisation a red cross on a white ground *(show picture)*. This was the reverse of his national Swiss flag.

Today the Red Cross is to be found wherever there is suffering due to war, earthquake, famine or flood. Refugees, sick people, and those without homes are all helped. What was started to help those wounded in war has now become a mighty organisation to help also in time of peace. Nearly every country in the world recognises the Red Cross. In some non-Christian parts the society is called the Red Crescent, but the same work is done.

Hymns
Love's a gift that's good and free   (SNS 46)
Sad, puzzled eyes of small, hungry children   (SNS 80)
Would you walk by on the other side   (CP 70)

Talk
(Show the pictures and/or models of the Coventry crosses.) Another example of good coming out of evil is represented by these pictures. Where is this ruined church to be found? (Part of the old cathedral at Coventry.) Today there is a fine new cathedral in Coventry, but some of the old one is left, too. How did the old cathedral come to be destroyed? (It was bombed during the 1939-45 war by German bombers.) Coventry suffered very badly the night the cathedral was hit. The Germans were hoping to destroy the armament factories around the city, but instead they bombed the centre of Coventry. The cathedral was entirely destroyed except for the spire. When Sir Basil Spence designed the new cathedral it was agreed that some of the ruin should be left. Two pieces of charred timber were found and used to make the large cross which can still be seen there. The small metal cross was made from the large nails which had been used to fasten together the great beams. Behind the simple stone altar are two words: 'FATHER FORGIVE'.

Many thousands of visitors go to Coventry to see the beautiful new cathedral and to walk among the ruins of the old. Some come from overseas; some from Germany: they all read that message on the wall: 'FATHER FORGIVE'.

Prayer
Heavenly Father, we are thinking today about those who lost their lives fighting in war. We thank you that so many showed courage and unselfishness, that amidst all the suffering there were many examples of kindness and caring. We think of those who were wounded, especially of those still suffering today.

We thank you that even out of great evil good things can come. We are glad that there are organisations like the Red Cross to bring hope and love in disaster areas.

We know that we must learn to forgive, as the people of Coventry learned. We remember that their words, 'Father forgive' were first spoken by Jesus as he hung dying on the cross. Help us to learn to forgive, too.

Hymns

Blow, wind, blow, wind   (SNS 44)

Spirit of God, as strong as the wind   (CP 63)

Follow-up for the class-room

1   Find out more about the work of the Red Cross in both war and peace. Find out if there is a local branch near your school. Invite a speaker to tell you more about their work.

2   Nursing and hospital care in this country was greatly improved because of Florence Nightingale's experience in another war. Find out about the Crimea and her part in relieving suffering there.

3   Discuss why imitation poppies are sold for Remembrance Day. What is the money collected used for? Prepare a poster showing how the poppies are made, and how the money collected from their sale is used.

4   One of the hardest things Jesus said was, 'Love your enemies'. Discuss the meaning of this; bear in mind that 'love' does not necessarily mean 'like'.

Sharing our gifts — 1

Note
The material for the following two assemblies is based on the story of Jonah. It is suggested that the two assemblies should be consecutive.

The Assembly

Preparation
Ask the children what we mean when we say we have received 'a gift'. (Ideas might include a present for birthday or Christmas.) Sometimes at football we say, 'That goal was a gift', meaning we did not have to try very hard to get it. Or we say, 'John is good at painting; it's a gift.' Or 'Jane is a gifted dancer.'

Ask what all these uses of the word have in common. (They are all things given to us. We do not have to pay for them or do anything special to get them.) But that does not mean that we do not have to do something with them after we have received them.

Talk: God's gift to the Jews
The Jews had been given a special gift by God. They had been chosen to be specially close to him so that they could learn about him and so understand what he wanted them to do. God spoke to their ancestors such as Abraham, Isaac and Jacob. He promised to make them into a great nation. God gave them laws through Moses so that they could learn to live good lives. He sent prophets such as Jeremiah and Isaiah to teach about how God's people should behave. They were a *chosen* people. It was a great gift. But very few understood that a gift has to be used for the good of all, not kept selfishly for oneself. One unknown Jew did understand that his people had been chosen for a purpose. He wrote a story to teach his fellow-Jews what that purpose was.

Story: Jonah the prophet

Jonah was a prophet: a man of God who ought to have obeyed God. One day God told Jonah to go to the great city of Nineveh to tell the people there that God had seen how wicked they were and that they must do something about their way of living.

Now these people were not Jews. Jonah did not see why God should bother about them at all. He decided he would not go; instead he would take a holiday and get away from God. Off he went to Joppa and boarded a boat for Spain. He was tired out with being pestered by God to do unpleasant things. He went below to sleep and forget his troubles.

But he could not get away from God so easily. God sent a great storm. The sailors became frightened; they were used to rough weather, but this storm seemed to be different. They were not Jews: Jews did not make good sailors. As the storm worsened, they threw some cargo overboard to lighten the ship. It did no good. The waves rose higher; the wind blew with even greater fury. It seemed that they were going to capsize. Nothing was left but prayer. Each man prayed to his own god for help. But where was that passenger? He should be praying, too. The crew needed all the help they could get.

The captain went below and found Jonah, still fast asleep. The captain shook him, 'Get up,' he shouted. 'Pray to your god, for we are all about to drown.'

But how could Jonah pray to God? He was running away from God!

The sailors' prayers seemed to be having no effect. The storm grew worse. In desperation the crew decided to draw lots to see who was responsible for such an unusual storm—and Jonah's name was drawn!

Jonah told them that he was a Jew who worshipped God who had made the earth and the sea. He was running away from God. The sailors were terrified; they knew that Jonah was wrong to do that. 'What must we do to you to stop the storm?' they asked Jonah.

Jonah did not hesitate. 'Throw me into the sea,' he replied. 'It is my fault that the storm has come. Throw me in and the sea will become calm.'

The sailors were good men and did not want to throw Jonah overboard. Instead they tried to row the ship towards shore but the fury of the storm continued to grow. They were in danger of breaking up at any moment. So they took Jonah and threw him into the boiling sea, praying that God would forgive them for the death of their passenger.

(From Jonah 1.1-16.)

Hymns
In Christ there is no east or west
We thank you, Lord, for giving us   (SNS 61)

Prayer
We thank you, Lord, for the gifts you have given to all of us; for our lives, our daily food, our health; for our families and friends and those who care for us.

We thank you for the special gifts you have given to some of us: to be able to talk well, or write good stories or poems, or understand mathematics. May we develop our gifts well.

We thank you for the ability to make things with our hands. May we be good workmen.

We are specially grateful for the gifts of sympathy, friendliness, generosity and helpfulness. May we use them every day and so make them grow.

Follow-up for the class-room

1   Prepare in small groups to share specific gifts at the second Assembly on 'Sharing our gifts'. For example, a group could rehearse music for introducing the Assembly; a group choose and practise a song; a group prepare a backcloth or background scenery for use during the conclusion of the Jonah story.

2   Jonah was really running away from his responsibility to share with others his gift of knowing God. He found it was not possible to run away. In a group, talk about what can happen if people shirk their responsibilities to share what God has given them.

3   Read the parable in Matthew 25.14-30 which is about using and sharing our gifts. Prepare the parable as a play, either for presentation at the second Assembly on 'Sharing our gifts' or for another suitable Assembly.

Sharing our gifts — 2

The Assembly

Preparation
See under 'Follow-up for the class-room' in the first Assembly 'Sharing our gifts'.

Sharing
A group plays the prepared music resulting from 'Sharing our gifts—1'.

Hymns
He's got the whole world in his hand   (CP 19)
This is the world that God has made   (SNS 8)
(A hymn, song, or verse may be sung as a solo or by a small choir as a result of 'Sharing our gifts—1'.)

Introduction
In our last assembly we were thinking about sharing our gifts. Today we have enjoyed listening to music played and sung: some have used their gifts to help us enjoy our worship. We develop our gifts by sharing them. We lose our gifts if we keep them selfishly to ourselves.

Story: Jonah the prophet *(continued)*
Jonah had been selfish. God had given the Jews a precious gift, to know him and love him. But they had thought that this meant that God cared only for them. When God wanted Jonah to take a message to the non-Jewish city of Nineveh, Jonah decided not to go. He boarded a ship travelling in the opposite direction. But a great storm arose, the sailors felt Jonah was responsible for it, and threw him overboard. Jonah

35

struggled for his life in the sea. Down, down, he went into the cold, green depths.

But God did not let him die. Along came a huge fish and swallowed Jonah. Into the dark, slimy, smelly fish's inside he went. He was breathless, shocked, spluttering, choking and coughing, but still alive. When he recovered his wits he started to pray. He had not been able to pray before, but now he could. Now he knew he could never escape from God because he found that God was with him even inside this fish. For three days he was there then, as the fish swam near the land, it spewed out Jonah onto the beach.

There he lay, more dead than alive. He was in no state to listen to God's demands. But that did not matter. Once again God told Jonah to go to Nineveh and warn them. This time Jonah did not argue; he went.

Nineveh was such a huge city that it took three days to cross it on foot. Now Jonah was in the centre, speaking God's message to the people. 'In forty days Nineveh will be destroyed. God has seen your wickedness and can ignore it no longer,' said Jonah. He expected the people either to ignore him or to make fun of him, but they did neither. To his surprise they listened. Everyone listened, from greatest to least; even the king listened. He ordered everyone in the land to fast and, to show how sorry they were for their evil ways, the king further ordered everyone—young and old, rich and poor, even the animals—to wear sackcloth. 'All must pray,' said the king. 'Perhaps God will listen and forgive us.' And so it was. God did forgive them and he did not punish them.

But was Jonah pleased? Not a bit of it! He was angry. 'I knew you would forgive them,' he said to God. 'That's why I ran away before. I knew you to be a merciful God.' And Jonah thought, 'Why should God forgive them? After all, they are not Jews. Why should God love them?'

Off he went into the desert to sulk. He built a shelter there and waited. Perhaps God would change his mind and teach these foreigners a lesson.

God gave Jonah a present. He made a plant grow up so tall and shady that it formed a sort of umbrella over his head to shield him from the fierce sun. Jonah dozed off. At dawn the plant that protected him shrivelled and died. The hot wind blew. The sun blazed down. Jonah felt faint. 'Let me die,' he moaned. Although he felt ill, he was really angry with God. After all he had suffered, even the poor plant had been taken from him and killed. It was then that God taught him the lesson which he had refused to learn.

'This plant grew up in a night and died the next,' said God. 'You did nothing for it, yet you are angry because it has died. You are sorry for the plant. How much more should I be sorry for the great city of Nineveh with more than 120,000 innocent children and many animals.'

(From Jonah 2—4)

The unknown Jewish author made up that story. He wanted the *chosen* people to know why they had been chosen: it was so that they could tell everyone about God and his love. The gift they had was to be shared, just as the gifts we are given are to be shared.

Reading
This beautiful psalm is a prayer for God's help; it also tells of God's love and willingness to forgive.

From the depths of my despair
   I call to you, Lord.
Hear my cry, O Lord;
   listen to my call for help!
If you kept a record of our sins,
   who could escape being condemned?
But you forgive us,
   so that we should stand in awe of you.

I wait eagerly for the Lord's help,
   and in his word I trust.
I wait for the Lord
   more eagerly than watchmen wait for the dawn—
   than watchmen wait for the dawn.

Israel, trust in the Lord,
   because his love is constant
   and he is always willing to save.
He will save his people Israel
   from all their sins.

(Psalm 130, GNB)

Hymns
I'll work for Jesus in the world   (SNS 68)
The King of love my shepherd is

Prayer

Forgive us, Lord, for the times when we have not done the things we know you want us to do: times when we have been unkind or unhelpful, times when we have made someone unhappy. Help us to understand what you want us to do, and then to obey you.

Follow-up for the class-room

1   Read Jonah 2.1-9. Verses 5 and 6 describe how it felt to Jonah to go down into the depths. His description is graphic and would make an excellent picture. Draw or paint it.

2   When Solomon became king after his father David died, he dreamed that God asked him what he would like to have as a gift. Read 2 Chronicles 1.7-12. What did Solomon ask for? If you had the chance to ask God for a gift, what would you choose, and why?

3   Gifts grow if they are used and shared. Think of something the group can do, as individuals or as a group, to help someone in need locally. Plan the undertaking, and carry it out as soon as possible.

Towards Christmas — 1

The Assembly

Preparation
Two children will need to learn and rehearse the drama, or be ready to read it.

Introduction
Most people keep their homes reasonably clean, but make a special effort when guests are expected. Is it like that in your home? What does your family do to prepare for guests? (Make everything spotless. Straighten out untidy corners. Arrange flowers. Prepare some special food.)

About three hundred and fifty years ago, a poet, whose name is unknown, wrote a poem on this theme. It is an Advent poem: a poem about the coming of Jesus. But, first of all, he imagines that a king is paying a visit to a rather splendid hall. What a flurry and bustle goes on! All the best things are brought out. Everything is made just right. Then, right at the end, the poet contrasts all that preparation for the king's visit with what happened when Jesus came.

Poem: Preparations
(The word 'dazie' in this poem means a canopy)

Yet if His Majesty, our sovereign lord,
Should of his own accord
Friendly himself invite,
And say 'I'll be your guest tomorrow night,'
How should we stir ourselves, call and command
All hands to work! 'Let no man idle stand!

'Set me fine Spanish tables in the hall;
See they be fitted all;

39

Let there be room to eat
And order taken that there want no meat,
See every sconce and candlestick made bright,
That without tapers they may give a light.

'Look to the presence: are the carpets spread,
The dazie o'er the head,
The cushions in the chairs,
And all the candles lighted on the stairs?
Perfume the chambers, and in any case
Let each man give attendance in his place!'

Thus, if a king were coming, would we do;
And 'twere good reason too;
For 'tis a duteous thing
To show all honour to an earthly king,
And after all our travail and our cost,
So he be pleased, to think no labour lost.

But at the coming of the King of Heaven
All's set at six and seven;
We wallow in our sin,
Christ cannot find a chamber in the inn.
We entertain him always like a stranger,
And, as at first, still lodge him in the manger.

Talk

For many hundreds of years the Jews had been expecting the Messiah to
come. Messiah is a Hebrew word which means anointed. Kings and
priests were anointed with oil. That is, some oil was poured on their
heads when they took office. This was to show that they had been given
a special task to do by God and also that he had given them special
powers with which to do it. But THE Messiah was thought of as being
very special amongst those set apart for God's work.

Reading

Listen to these verses from the book of the prophet Isaiah which many
people believe tell of the coming Messiah.

A child is born to us!
   A son is given to us!

And he will be our ruler.
He will be called, 'Wonderful Counsellor',
  'Mighty God', 'Eternal Father',
  'Prince of Peace'.
His royal power will continue to grow;
  his kingdom will always be at peace.
He will rule as King David's successor,
  basing his power on right and justice,
  from now until the end of time.

(Isaiah 9.6-7, GNB)

Drama
Let us imagine we are interviewing a Jew, called Simon—a common
Jewish name—in the streets of Jerusalem a few years before Jesus was
born, when the Jewish people were under the harsh rule of the Romans.

Interviewer: May I ask you, Simon, when you expect Messiah to come?
Simon (glancing round cautiously): Before I answer any of your questions, let
me make it crystal clear that if you are a Roman spy, my Zealot friends
will know what to do about it.
Interviewer: You can speak freely to me. I have no love for the Romans. I
am a Greek and most of my family are slaves in Italy . . . and I know all
about your Zealot friends' skill with the knife!
Simon: Good! Just so long as you don't let it slip your mind. Now about
Messiah. He will come very soon. Any day now.
Interviewer: What will he be like?
Simon (boasting): He will be the mightiest hero of all time. He will be of
King David's family; but he will be greater than David ever was.
Interviewer: In what way?
Simon: He will raise a great army and throw these Roman tyrants into the
sea. The people are sick of paying taxes to these robbers. They are sick of
seeing the lines of crosses along the roads where men have been executed
as a warning to others to toe the line. They are sick of feeding and
housing the rag-bag army of Roman mercenaries drawn from the gutters
of the Empire.
Interviewer: Your Messiah will have to be a pretty tough character to do all
that!
Simon: How can he fail? He is God's anointed one. But that isn't all.
Interviewer: Surely that's more than enough to be going on with!

Simon: Oh, no! Jerusalem will become the centre of the world. Messiah will reign there as king. All lesser kings will come to Jerusalem to bow down before him and do him honour. In the temple, God will be praised every minute of the day as multitudes of priests offer sacrifice. Peace will reign everywhere. Crops will flourish. Sickness will vanish from the earth. It will be the start of a new age.

Interviewer: It sounds perfect . . . but will it ever happen?

Hymns
O come, O come, Immanuel
The eternal Lord of earth and sky   (SNS 22)

Comment
The gospel record certainly suggests that Jesus was a descendant of David. But Jesus was like no earthly king. He made no attempt to raise a rebellion. He taught forgiveness of enemies, even of the Romans! He praised the meek and called them blessed. He went about doing good, seeking out and helping the poor and the sick. This was the Messiah, God's anointed one.

Prayer
We thank you, God, that Jesus came to show us what you are like and to teach us how to live. We remember that when he came no one was prepared to receive him. He was born in a stable, one of the very poor, and soon he became a refugee, fleeing for his life. Most people were not prepared to receive his word. May we prepare our hearts for the coming of Jesus this Christmas time.

Follow-up for the class-room

1 Make an Advent Calendar large enough to use as a wall poster. This can be very simple, or more elaborate according to the imagination and capabilities of the group. An Advent Calendar is made by sticking together two pieces of paper or card the same size. On the top sheet are

24 'doors', one for each day in December to Christmas Eve, which, when opened, reveal small pictures related to Christmas. Old Christmas cards are a useful source for the pictures.

2 Make a crib, modelling the figures from clay, wood or paper, etc, and setting them in a stable scene.

3 Have a Christmas Quiz. Useful source books are *The Christmas Book* (NCEC) and *The Stories of our Christmas Customs* (Ladybird).

Towards Christmas — 2

Note:
It is suggested that this Assembly follows on from 'Towards Christmas—1'

The Assembly

Introduction
Invite the children to tell of Christmas preparations which they are making. (Buying and sending cards, making and packing presents, decorating homes and trees, etc.) There always seems to be a rush as we get near Christmas, however early we start preparations. This modern poem tells of the bustle of the days before Christmas.

Saturday before Christmas
All the busy folk today
   Are part of heaven,
Though they forget it often
   Or do not know it, even.
All the people selling things,
   All the people buying;
All the people packing things,
   Wrapping, tying;
All the coach and bus men,
   All the railway host;
All the men who gather
   and carry the post;
All the bustling housewives,
   Cooking, cleaning;
All the very practical
   With no time for dreaming:
Because they help each other,

Because they serve goodwill,
They all go together
   To Bethlehem's hill.
They may forget it often,
   They may not know it, even,
But all the busy folk today
   Are part of heaven.
All of them are brothers;
   Pray that each may know
A little time of quiet
   To find that it is so.

(Lilian Cox)

Talk
During the few days before Jesus was born, all was bustle, too. A census ordered by the Romans meant that Jesus' parents had to make a long trip from their home in Nazareth to be registered in Joseph's home town of Bethlehem, the 'city of David'. On the night of their arrival, Jesus was born. At that time, few people had any idea that he was the Messiah.

When Jesus was grown-up, he chose a group of disciples to be with him in his work. He went about doing good, seeking out the poor and sick, and helping them. One day he asked his disciples a question.

Readings
Then Jesus and his disciples went away to the villages near Caesarea Philippi. On the way he asked them, 'Tell me, who do people say I am?'

'Some say that you are John the Baptist,' they answered; 'others say that you are Elijah, while others say that you are one of the prophets.'

'What about you?' he asked them. 'Who do you say I am?'

Peter answered, 'You are the Messiah.'

(Mark 8.27-29, GNB)

Jesus accepted the title of Messiah or Christ. Many people now believe that these verses from the prophet Isaiah told of the coming Messiah—a very different kind of Messiah from that expected by most Jews.

'We despised him and rejected him;
  he endured suffering and pain.
No one would even look at him—
  we ignored him as if he were nothing.

He was arrested and sentenced and led off to die,
  and no one cared about his fate.
He was put to death for the sins of our people.
He was placed in a grave with evil men,
  he was buried with the rich,
even though he had never committed a crime
  or ever told a lie.'

(Isaiah 53.3, 8-9, GNB)

These verses form a picture of one who would suffer and die. He is called the Suffering Servant. Jesus knew these words very well and in his life and death he *became* that one whom the prophet said would come.

Prayer
We thank you, God, that Jesus came as a suffering servant to show us what you are like and to teach us how to live. He is your gift to us. Through Jesus we learn how much you care for us and love us. We remember that those who would follow Jesus must learn from his example. Christmas is a time for giving and receiving gifts. We enjoy receiving gifts from those we love. Help us to give gifts, too—gifts of helping and caring, so that Christmas joy may be all round us.

Hymns
Good people all   (SNS 24)
Go, tell it on the mountain   (CP 24)

Follow-up for the class-room

1   Find and read two other references to the coming of Messiah: Jeremiah 23.5 and Ezekiel 34.23-24. Look up Jeremiah and Ezekiel in a

46

Bible dictionary to find out when they lived and something about their lives.

2   The reading from Isaiah provided some of the words for Handel's *The Messiah*. Read in the *Authorised Version* (which Handel used) Isaiah 53.3-6. Find and play the parts of *The Messiah* which use these verses.

3   Write words for a new carol, either using a well-known carol tune or composing a new tune.

4   Tell the story of Christmas from the point of view of a shepherd boy in the fields near Bethlehem, or the innkeeper's son. Reference: Luke 2.1-20.

Treasure hunters

The Assembly

Preparation
Have ready to display some personal 'treasure' found in a junk shop or on a market stall.

Introduction
Most people are fascinated by treasure, whether reading about it in books such as *Treasure Island* by R.L.Stevenson or hearing about the old Tudor objects that were found in and around the *Mary Rose,* Henry VIII's flagship, raised from the sea-bed in 1982, four hundred years after it sank.

Story
Mr and Mrs Green—John and Julie—were treasure hunters. They did not go off to tropical islands looking for pirates' treasure, but they did love looking in junk shops and going to flea markets. *(Show your own 'treasure' and tell how you found it.)*

John and Julie did not know much about antiques but they lived in hope that they might pick up a real treasure for a few pounds which would turn out to be priceless.

One day they heard that a firm of auctioneers from London was holding a valuation day in a local hall. People could take along their treasures and the experts would value them free of charge. Julie and her husband decided to go, taking a few of the treasures they had collected over the years. 'And let's take that old pot your grandmother gave us,' said Julie.

'What, that old vase we use as an umbrella stand?' said John. 'It's got a crack right down one side. I've been thinking of throwing it out.'

'Well, it'll be a bit of fun,' said Julie. 'Let's clean it up a bit.'

So they took the sticks and umbrellas out of the old pot and gave it a wash. 'It's really quite pretty now you can see it properly,' said Julie. The vase was covered with blue flowers against a white background.

When they reached the hall it was crowded. A young man was dealing with the pottery items. At other tables people were showing paintings, jewellery, guns, furniture. One lady was carrying a huge stuffed bear that was leaving a trail of sawdust behind it.

The young man did not seem to be impressed with what he had seen so far, but he did his best to smother a yawn. Then it was John and Julie's turn. They wanted him to look at their real treasures first but clearly that was not what he wanted. Suddenly he became very alert. He stared at the blue and white vase. Trying to suppress the urgent note in his voice he said, 'Would you mind if I had a look at this first?' He examined it with great care, saying nothing. He turned it round. He tut-tutted at the large crack. Then he called a friend over to look. They talked quietly together for a time. Then the young man turned to the Greens. 'This could be valuable,' he said. 'May I take it away to do some research on it?'

'Yes,' said Julie, 'but what do you think it is?'

'I'd rather not say now,' he replied. 'Give me a week or so.'

About ten days later the Greens heard that the vase had been examined by other experts. It was Chinese, early Ming, and worth at least £12,000, even in its chipped and cracked condition.

The vase was auctioned some months later in London at a very exclusive auction room for £13,500. 'Just think,' said Julie to her husband, 'we're always looking for treasure and we've been living with one right under our noses for over thirty years!'

'Yes, and keeping umbrellas in it,' said John.

Hymns
As the bridegroom to his chosen   (Partners in Praise)
Merchant, merchant, what do you seek   (SNS 36)

Reading
Many people would give almost anything to be able to meet Jesus and talk to him. As the next best thing they may look for him in books: they read about him in the gospels; they go to church and join in services. We do learn about Jesus in these ways, but that is not the same as really meeting him. Is it possible to meet him? Jesus said it was.

'When the Son of Man comes as King and all the angels with him, he will sit on his royal throne, and the people of all the nations will be gathered before him. Then he will divide them into two groups, just as a shepherd separates the sheep from the goats. He will put the righteous people on his right and the others on his left. Then the King will say to the people on his right, "Come, you that are blessed by my Father! Come and possess the kingdom which has been prepared for you ever since the creation of the world. I was hungry and you fed me, thirsty and you gave me a drink; I was a stranger and you received me in your homes, naked and you clothed me; I was sick and you took care of me, in prison and you visited me."

'The righteous will then answer him, "When, Lord, did we ever see you hungry and feed you, or thirsty and give you a drink? When did we ever see you a stranger and welcome you in our homes, or naked and clothe you? When did we ever see you sick or in prison, and visit you?" The King will reply, "I tell you, whenever you did this for one of the least important of these brothers of mine, you did it for me!" '

(Matthew 25.31-40, GNB)

In this story Jesus was telling his listeners—and us—that we meet him in the people round us, and especially in those who are in need of our love and care.

Hymns
Oh, how we love to laugh and sing   (SNS 76)
When I needed a neighbour, were you there   (CP 65)

Prayer
Heavenly Father, we are so busy looking for happiness through things which we have not got that we fail to find happiness in things close to us. We often think of Jesus as living so long ago that we fail to see him in the people we meet every day and especially those who need our help. Father, forgive our foolishness, and help us to recognise real treasure when it is close to us.

Follow-up for the class-room

1   Jesus told two very short parables about treasure. Read them in Matthew 13.44 and Matthew 13.45-46. Discuss what Jesus was meaning to teach through these stories.

2   Encourage the children to use a concordance to discover New Testament references to 'treasure'. Each child should choose one reference and memorise it.

3   At her coronation, the queen was given a Bible which was described as 'the greatest treasure'. Find out why this is part of the coronation ceremony, and why the Bible is described in this way.

4   Try to discover people in need in the immediate neighbourhood, and work out ways of meeting their needs.

Facing difficulties

The Assembly

Preparation
Ask several children to be prepared to read out from the *Guinness Book of Records* a record-breaking achievement that required great determination and perseverance.

Display a picture of the Australian dingo.

Introduction
From time to time we all have to face difficulties in our lives. Some people *choose* to bring difficulties upon themselves by attempting to break records. *(Ask the children to read their excerpts.)*

These record-breaking efforts required courage to overcome exhaustion and weakness. But, of course, the people concerned could always give up. They *chose* that particular difficulty.

We do not choose the difficulties that come to us. That is what makes them hard. *(Ask the children if they have had to face a difficulty recently. Examples could be going to the dentist, going to hospital, taking an examination, having to own up to some wrongdoing, realising we cannot do something we want to do, losing a loved pet.)* Some difficulties are even harder to face than these. Some people are handicapped and have to accept that they will remain so for the rest of their lives. Sometimes we lose someone in our family whom we love very dearly.

Story: Facing the flames
One of the worst hazards of the dry forests of Australia is fire. The great trees may manage to survive all but the worst fires but below them the small trees, bushes and shrubs burn easily. Hardly any rain falls in the summer and fires are easily started. Most of the birds are safe enough: they can escape. Most animals can manage fairly well as long as the wind

does not become too strong: they can run away from the fire.

But as the speed of the wind increases from ten miles per hour to twenty miles per hour, some of the slow-moving animals are overtaken by the fire. The koala bear and the possum suffer. Then as the wind rises, the fire travels faster: thirty miles an hour, forty miles an hour. Then even quite quick animals such as rabbits and wallabies will be killed as the greedy flames overtake them. When the wind rises to gale force even the great kangaroos that travel very fast indeed will be overtaken and killed.

Only one animal manages to survive the worst fires blown by the great winds: the dingo, the small, yellow, wild dog of Australia. The dingo crouches down *facing* the flames as they rush onwards. As the flames get nearer and nearer, the dingo remains crouching on all-fours. The heat is intense and the noise of burning brushwood and timber is quite deafening. Then the flames are upon the dingo. He jumps up and dashes right through the flames. The fire is only a fairly narrow strip, and behind the burning margin lies the burned-out bush, smouldering and black. The dingo emerges, singed a little, but alive. He has survived not by running away but by facing the danger head on.

Hymns
Life is like a journey   (SNS 67)
The journey of life   (CP 45)

Reading
St Paul had a serious illness. We are not sure just what it was, but he felt that it was holding him back in his work of spreading the gospel. If only he could be rid of it how much more he would be able to do! In his second letter to the church at Corinth, Paul wrote:

But to keep me from being puffed up with pride because of the many wonderful things I saw, I was given a painful physical ailment, which acts as Satan's messenger to beat me and keep me from being proud. Three times I prayed to the Lord about this and asked him to take it away. But his answer was: 'My grace is all you need, for my power is strongest when you are weak.' I am most happy, then, to be proud of my weaknesses, in order to feel the protection of Christ's power over me. I am content with weaknesses, insults, hardships, persecutions, and difficulties for Christ's sake. For when I am weak, then I am strong.

(2 Corinthians 12.7-10, GNB)

Paul faced his problem, accepted his weakness, and made it work for the glory of God. Whatever our difficulty may be, it never helps to run away from it. If we face it, unpleasant though it may seem, we can come through. We can ask God to help us to face our difficulties and maybe, like Paul, we will come to see that they have some value, too.

Prayer
Lord, you know that we are often afraid. We fear being hurt. We fear being alone. We often do wrong things because we are frightened to go against our friends. We sometimes lie to avoid punishment. Help us to face up to our difficulties, and be with us when we are tested.

Reading
God is our shelter and strength,
    always ready to help in times of trouble.
So we will not be afraid, even if the earth is shaken
    and mountains fall into the ocean depths;
even if the seas roar and rage,
    and the hills are shaken by the violence.

(Psalm 46.1-3, GNB)

Hymn
My faith, it is an oaken staff

Follow-up for the class-room

1   Find out how people can be helped to face the great difficulty of blindness. Discover what aids are available for blind people (eg, from the

Royal National Institute for the Blind catalogue of aids for the blind).
Look up the story of Louis Braille.

2   St Paul was once an enemy of the new Christian church. He was
present when Stephen was stoned to death. Read about how he became a
Christian, in Acts 9.1-9. From his letters, list and find the locations of
some of the churches which he started in spite of many difficulties.

3   Most children will know someone who is handicapped in some way.
Ask them to write about how he or she manages to overcome his or her
difficulties.

4   Ask each child to write about a difficulty he or she has had to face, eg,
going into hospital, facing a bully, having a great disappointment, facing
the death of a pet. What helped to overcome the difficulty?

5   Read Psalm 23 which tells how God helped the poet to face his
difficulties. Learn the psalm by heart.

Hearing—and hearing!

The Assembly

Preparation
Select a record or tape of a piece of music which has instrumental variety, eg, *The Overture to HMS Pinafore* (Gilbert and Sullivan), or *The Young Person's Guide to the Orchestra* (Benjamin Britten).

Obtain a drawing of the middle ear or enlarge the diagram.

Choose readers for the Bible reading.

Hymn
Sounds of music: rock or ballad   (SNS 6)

Talk
Invite the children to say what a hammer is, and what it is used for. *(Put up the hammer picture, commenting that this is a special kind of hammer. Repeat with anvil and stirrup.)* These are all parts of the body: where are they found?

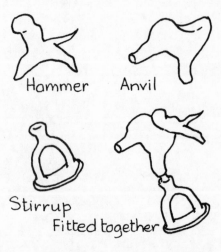

Sounds enter the external ear and strike against the ear-drum making it vibrate. The ear-drum separates the middle ear from the external ear. The middle ear is a tiny cavity filled with air. Inside there is a chain of tiny bones linked to one another: they are called the hammer, the anvil, and the stirrup.

The hammer bone is fastened by its handle to the drum and by its head to the anvil bone; this in turn is fitted to the arch of the stirrup bone; and the foot of the stirrup fits into the oval window which communicates with the inner ear. *(Put up diagram of how they fit together.)* Sound waves set the drum vibrating and these connected bones carry the vibrations across the middle ear to the inner ear. The stirrup bone goes up and down in the oval window like a plunger. The inner ear is a small bag filled with fluid. The fluid is stirred by the movement of the stirrup bone. Little hairs are made to move and stimulate the hearing or auditory nerve which takes the stimulus to the hearing centre of the brain. Here vibrations become electrical impulses and we say we hear something.

Ears are wonderful things. When we listen to music we can tell whether a flute is playing, or a violin or a trumpet: each instrument has a different vibration pattern. Listen to this music. *(Play the selected pieces—see Preparation.)*

Ask which instruments could be heard. For sounds to mean something to us we have to be able to learn from experience. You recognised string sounds in the music because you have heard the sound before. You have seen what makes such sounds; you have been told its name; you remember all this. If you hear the word 'dog' you know what it means because you associate the sound with particular animals. But if someone said 'chien' you would hear a sound which would mean nothing unless you knew some French, for 'chien' is the French word for 'dog'. Hearing and understanding are quite different. We hear with our ears, but there is another way of hearing, too. We can describe it as hearing with our mind.

Reading
Jesus once said, 'You have ears — can't you hear?' In the Old Testament there is a story which illustrates this.

Voice 1: In those days, when the boy Samuel was serving the Lord under the direction of Eli, there were very few messages from the Lord, and visions from him were quite rare. One night Eli, who was now almost blind, was sleeping in his own room; Samuel was sleeping in the sanctuary, where the sacred Covenant Box was. Before dawn, while the lamp was still burning, the Lord called Samuel.

Voice 2: He answered, 'Yes, sir!' and ran to Eli and said, 'You called me, and here I am.'

But Eli answered, 'I didn't call you; go back to bed.' So Samuel went back to bed.

Voice 1: The Lord called Samuel again. The boy did not know that it was the Lord, because the Lord had never spoken to him before.

Voice 2: So he got up, went to Eli, and said, 'You called me, and here I am.'

But Eli answered, 'My son, I didn't call you; go back to bed.'

Voice 1: The Lord called Samuel a third time; he got up, went to Eli, and said, 'You called me, and here I am.'

Then Eli realised that it was the Lord who was calling the boy, so he said to him, 'Go back to bed; and if he calls you again, say, "Speak, Lord, your servant is listening." ' So Samuel went back to bed.

Voice 2: The Lord came and stood there, and called as he had before, 'Samuel! Samuel!'

Samuel answered, 'Speak; your servant is listening.'

(1 Samuel 3.1-10, GNB)

Comment

From that time on, Samuel became God's boy in a very real sense. As he grew he learned to pray, listening and speaking to God as he led his people.

God speaks to people in many different ways. Often God speaks and we do not listen—because we do not want to hear. Hearing may make us uncomfortable. For example, we may hear about someone who needs help, but we turn a deaf ear: it may cost us time or money or effort to help that person. We have heard God speaking, but we have not listened.

Jesus said that when we help others we are helping him. Perhaps he uses the voices of lonely people, sick people, starving people, in different parts of the world, in order to speak to us.

Hymns

Hushed was the evening hymn
In the morning early   (CP 60)

Prayer

Heavenly Father, we thank you for the wonderful world of sound, and for your gift of hearing. We can hear the sounds of nature—running water, bird song, waves on the shore and wind in the trees. We can hear the sounds of music, the voices of our friends and family.

May we be willing to listen to your voice, however we may hear it, and obey, even though obeying may cost us a good deal. We know that in giving we shall receive, and in serving we shall be satisfied. *So may we show your glory to the world, by the way we life. L.P.*

Follow-up for the class-room

1 Think of different kinds of music; play a selection with as much variety as possible. Discuss with the group whether they think God can speak to people through music and, if so, how.

2 Poets who wrote the psalms often spoke of feeling God's presence in mountains and hills. Read Psalm 36.6 and Psalm 148.7-10. Find other psalms which express God's presence in nature. Encourage the children each to write a poem about how God speaks to him/her in nature.

3 Have a class discussion about how God speaks to us through other people. Read Matthew 25.31-40 and 41-45.

4 Read Genesis 1.26-30. Discuss what this tells us about our responsibility towards living things. Ask whether God speaks to us through animals and their needs.

Seeing—and seeing!

The Assembly

Preparation
Obtain an optician's chart or make a similar board diagram. On card, make the following notice, large enough to be seen by everyone, but keep it hidden until needed:

```
KEEP OFF THE
THE GRASS
```

Introduction
You may think that in order to see, all you have to do is open your eyes. But we have to *learn* how to use our eyes. A new-born baby cannot focus its eyes; it has to learn how to do this.

Show the sight-testing chart. Ask the children to explain what it is used for. Ask how many are able to read the bottom line of it. Comment that even though they may have perfect vision, as judged by this test, they may not always see things correctly.

Display the notice. Ask several children to read it. In nearly every case 'the' will be read once only. Explain that this is because the brain tells us what *ought* to be there. We are used to seeing 'Keep off the grass', so we do not see all the words. But there is even more to seeing than that.

Story
John was bored. He was staying with his aunt and uncle for a week in their cottage just outside Salisbury, close to some lovely wooded country. He had read his comic at least six times. Now he was gazing through the window at the sunny garden and the fields beyond. He was not used to the country and Uncle Bill and Aunty Peggy had no children of their own so there was no one to play with. Nothing ever seemed to happen in

the country.

Suddenly the whole garden burst into life. A black cat streaked across the lawn and pounced on the small birds feeding near the bird table. With shrill cries of alarm the birds scattered. But one was too slow and the cat seized it in its mouth and made off towards the nearest bushes.

John acted. He opened the french window and dashed across the lawn yelling and flapping his arms wildly. The cat, startled, dropped the bird and fled for its life.

Gently John picked up the floppy little brown body. The bird looked dead. Then it began to stir and make faint chirping noises. Carefully John placed it on the grass but it made no attempt to fly away.

'If I leave it here,' thought John, 'that cat will soon be back for it.' So he took the bird indoors. 'Look, Aunty,' he said, 'I've got a wounded sparrow.'

'Drat that old cat,' said Aunty Peggy. 'That's the second this week.'

'What shall I do with it?' asked John. 'It's not dead.'

'Put it in this box. When your uncle comes home he'll know what to do. He knows a lot about birds.'

That evening, Uncle Bill examined the little body carefully. The bird lay on its back on the palm of his hand very quietly as if it trusted him. Gently Uncle Bill extended its wings and felt along the fragile legs. 'I think it will get better,' he said. 'It's just shocked. Do you know what it is?'

'It's a sparrow,' said John.

'Yes, it's called a sparrow, but not the ordinary kind. It's a hedge sparrow, a dunnock. It's no relation to the ordinary house sparrow at all.' Uncle Bill showed John its slatey blue-grey head and chest. Now John could see it was really quite different from the sparrows that hopped about his garden at home.

That was the start of a great adventure of discovery for John. He began to *look* at the birds in the garden. Uncle Bill lent him a pair of binoculars and a book full of coloured pictures of birds. Soon, with some help, he was able to identify all kinds of birds that visited the garden and nearby fields. There were blackbirds, thrushes, blue tits, greenfinches, chaffinches, bullfinches, robins, wrens, house sparrows and, of course, dunnocks. There were birds he had never seen before—not really *seen* although they must have been there all the time. He began to keep a diary and to sketch some of the birds.

Oh, by the way, the frightened dunnock did get better. John was allowed to set it free next day and off it flew out of his hands.

Reading

Jesus once said:

'You have eyes—can't you see? You have ears—can't you hear?'

They came to Bethsaida, where some people brought a blind man to Jesus and begged him to touch him. Jesus took the blind man by the hand and led him out of the village. After spitting on the man's eyes, Jesus placed his hands on him and asked, 'Can you see anything?'

The man looked up and said, 'Yes, I can see people, but they look like trees walking about.'

Jesus again placed his hands on the man's eyes. This time the man looked intently, his eyesight returned, and he saw everything clearly.

(Mark 8.18, 22-25, GNB)

Comment

Jesus sometimes cured blind people, as in this story. But he was doing more than helping people to see again with their eyes. That is one way of seeing, but Jesus reminded his hearers that there is another way of seeing, too. We can describe it as seeing with our mind—using our mind's eye.

Some of the Jewish leaders said that Jesus was wicked, and that he went about doing evil, not good. These leaders were blind; they did not want to see the truth. We can be blind in this way, too. Jesus said, 'You have eyes—can't you see?'

Hymns

For the beauty of the earth
He gave me eyes so I could see   (CP 18)
Think of a world without any flowers   (CP 17)
When I see the trees so tall   (SNS 5)

Prayer

Heavenly Father, help us to see the beauty which is all around us. May we delight in all its variety: the many different birds and animals, the myriads of insects, the countless plants—all share their lives with us, and you have made them all.

Help us to be aware of the people around us. Open our eyes so that we can see those who need our love. Open our minds so that we can know how best to help them, and open our hands to do your work in the world.

Follow-up for the class-room

1   Make a bird diary based on observations either in school or at home. Note names of birds, their size, colour and any special features, such as song and way of moving.

2   Collect natural objects such as rocks and minerals, shells, bark, ferns, garden flowers. Make careful drawings of them. A hand lens will help many fine details to be seen. Wild flowers should not be picked, but drawings of them can be made in their natural habitat.

3   Provide some examples of optical illusions, and let the children 'prove' that they are illusions. Here is one example:

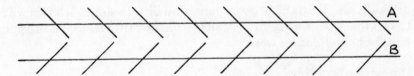

Are the lines A and B parallel?

4   Discuss how eyes can be used in school to pick up clues that show people are unhappy or in need of help. Think together about what could be done to help.

Being tempted

The Assembly

Preparation
Adults or older children should rehearse the dramatic reading.

Introduction
A dictionary gives the following meanings for the word 'Tempt': to put on trial, to test, to persuade to evil.

Everyone is tempted from time to time. It is part of being human. In many of the things we have to do there are right ways and wrong ways of behaving. This was true for Jesus, too. Right at the beginning of his work he had to think long and hard about how he would act in order to do God's will. It was not easy for him. God did not simply tell him what to do. Jesus went away to be quiet, without distractions, in order to prepare himself for his work.

Dramatised reading
Voice 1: Jesus returned from the Jordan full of the Holy Spirit and was led by the Spirit into the desert, where he was tempted by the Devil for forty days. In all that time he ate nothing, so that he was hungry when it was over.

Voice 2: If you are God's Son, order this stone to turn into bread.

Voice 3: The scripture says, 'Man cannot live on bread alone.'

Voice 1: Then the Devil took him up and showed him in a second all the kingdoms of the world.

Voice 2: I will give you all this power and all this wealth. It has all been handed over to me, and I can give it to anyone I choose. All this will be yours, then, if you worship me.

Voice 3: The scripture says, 'Worship the Lord your God and serve only him.'

Voice 1: Then the Devil took him to Jerusalem and set him on the highest point of the Temple, and said to him,

Voice 2: If you are God's Son, throw yourself down from here. For the scripture says, 'God will order his angels to take good care of you.' It also says, 'They will hold you up with their hands so that not even your feet will be hurt on the stones.'
Voice 3: The scripture says, 'Do not put the Lord your God to the test.'
Voice 1: When the Devil finished tempting Jesus in every way, he left him for a while.

(Adapted from Luke 4.1-13, GNB)

Talk

The first temptation was for Jesus to turn stones into bread, and so satisfy his hunger after fasting for so long. He was tempted to use his power to help himself. This he never did. Much later, when he was hanging on the cross, people jeered at him, asking why he did not help himself.

In the second temptation, the fact that Jesus could see all the world in a second tells us that the temptations were in his own mind. He wanted to win the world. He could do it by using power. Once he was ruling the world, think of all the good he could do. But again this would be a wrong use of power. He was to show God's power in a quite different way.

In the third temptation Jesus imagined being on the topmost point of the temple, and jumping down without harming himself. This was to do with power as well: to show his power in such a way would surely make people follow him. But Jesus did not want to *make* people follow. He wanted to win people by love. He wanted them to be free to make up their own minds.

At the end of the story the Devil leaves him . . . but only for a while. Jesus was to be tempted again. He had to struggle to the very end, but he did not give way.

There is nothing wrong in being tempted to do something evil; it is only wrong when we give in and do the evil thing.

Hymns

Growing, growing   (SNS 62)
One more step along the world I go   (CP 47)

Story

Bill, John and Fred were members of the Green Street gang—they were the *only* members of the gang. They all went to the same Middle School.

They were all in the same class. They had all come from the same First School two years earlier. In fact, as Bill said, they always seemed to have been together and to have done the same things. Perhaps the chief difference between them was that Fred's father no longer lived with him and his mother. He had left about two years before. Fred and his mother got on fine; she did not fuss too much but she was always there when Fred wanted her. It was hard at times because they didn't have very much money to spare: his father was supposed to pay something but he never did. Every Saturday morning Mum gave Fred his pocket money. She always said the same thing: 'Sorry it's not much.' Fred understood. She didn't earn much at her job.

One day the gang met in the old shed at the bottom of Bill's garden. They were going to have a feast. Fred brought out three chocolate biscuits his mother had given him. John produced a large bottle of fizzy drink. Bill's pockets were bulging. Slowly he produced an expensive block of chocolate, then a packet of marshmallows, and then several packets of nuts.

'Gosh!' said John. 'Your Dad won the pools or something?'

'No,' said Bill, hesitating a little. 'I'll tell you later. Let's eat first!' When they had finished the lot, Bill said, 'Now I'll tell you where they came from.' The others waited expectantly. 'You know that sweet shop in the High Street, near the lights? Well, it's changed hands. There's an old woman in the shop now, and she can't see much. All you do is go in with someone, then ask for something, and while she's serving you, your mate grabs things and stuffs them in his pockets. It's dead easy.'

'What if you get caught?' said John. 'My Dad would kill me.'

'You needn't worry about that,' said Bill. 'She's too slow. You could always dash out. By the time she got round the counter you'd be miles away.' There was a silence. 'She's got toys, too,' went on Bill. 'Well, what do you say?'

'I'll have a go,' said John. 'When shall we do it?'

'What do you think, Fred?' asked Bill. 'Shall we have a go tonight?'

Fred didn't reply. He was having a battle with himself. He was always short of money. It would be great to have plenty of sweets and toys. He could even sell some and give his mother the money: there were plenty of boys and girls with money to spare.

'Come on,' said Bill with an edge to his voice. 'You're not scared, are you?'

'Course not,' said Fred. 'I'm as brave as you any day of the week.'

'Prove it then,' said John. 'Come with us tonight.'

Being in the gang meant so much to Fred. If he refused to help this time he knew for certain he would be out. He was just about to say, 'Yes,

I'll see you tonight.' His mouth was already forming the first word. He stopped. In his mind's eye he saw his mother. She would be terribly hurt if she found out that he was a thief. But she wouldn't find out, would she? Then he thought, 'It isn't just what Mum would think. I would hate myself, too. I would know about it.'

'I'm going home,' said Fred. 'I think it's wrong to cheat the shopkeeper.' He left as quickly as he could. The sounds of jeers and laughter followed him. Bill and John wouldn't want anything to do with him now. But Fred wasn't sorry. At least he could look his mother in the eye and not feel guilty. And more, he had fought and won a battle with himself. But it had not been easy.

Hymns
All my thought, my Father God   (SNS 19)
He who would valiant be
When we're thinking what to do   (SNS 20)

Prayer
Lord, you understand what it means to be tempted; help us when we are put to the test. You had to struggle to do the right; help us to follow your example. We can be tempted in so many ways. We are tempted to be lazy. We are tempted to put ourselves first. We are tempted to hurt those weaker than ourselves. We are tempted to be dishonest. In all our temptations be with us, Lord, and help us to do what is right.

Follow-up for the class-room

1   Read the story of the temptations of Jesus, in Luke 4.1-13. Look at the three answers Jesus gave to the Devil. What do they have in common? One of the ways Jesus was helped to overcome temptation was through his knowledge of the scriptures. Jesus' answers all come from the book of Deuteronomy: 6.13; 8.3 and 6.16. Read these verses. Each child should make a chart in three columns showing (1) How Jesus was tempted; (2) What he/she thinks the temptation meant; and (3) Jesus' reply, and where he was quoting from.

2   Read and dramatise the temptation story in Genesis 3.1-6. The story is a kind of parable about how evil came into the world.

The good shepherd

The Assembly

Music
J.S.Bach: *Sheep may safely graze*

Introduction
The title of that music was *Sheep may safely graze*, by J.S.Bach. In this passage from the Bible, Jesus tells us about a shepherd in his own land. Look out for the differences between the way a shepherd worked then, and the way a shepherd works in our country.

Reading
Jesus said, 'I am telling you the truth: the man who does not enter the sheepfold by the gate, but climbs in some other way, is a thief and a robber. The man who goes in through the gate is the shepherd of the sheep. The gatekeeper opens the gate for him; the sheep hear his voice as he calls his own sheep by name, and he leads them out. When he has brought them out, he goes ahead of them, and the sheep follow him, because they know his voice. They will not follow someone else; instead, they will run away from such a person, because they do not know his voice.'

(John 10.1-5, GNB)

Comment
Did you spot the differences? The Jewish shepherd calls his sheep by name. He leads them and they follow him. The sheep recognise his voice.

There is no mention of dogs or rounding up. The Jewish way of treating sheep makes them seem much more intelligent than sheep here

68

that are driven. Here, sheep are treated as a flock and they are expected to act as a crowd.

Talk

One of the strangest sights in nature is animals suddenly following each other rushing straight to their deaths. Lemmings are small arctic rodents something like field mice. They gather in hundreds of thousands and travel long distances together—then dash into the sea and drown. No one is quite sure why they do this. It is almost as though in the huge crowd of animals the lemmings have no will of their own. Normally an animal will go to great lengths to preserve its life.

A similar thing happens to an animal at the other end of the size scale. The huge whale seems to have a similar fatal urge at times. Whales have stranded themselves in large numbers on sandbanks or beaches where they flounder quite unable to help themselves. When they are hauled back into deep water by well-meaning humans, they often undo the good work by returning later to die on the beaches.

Sheep have been known to behave in a similar way. One large flock in France followed a frightened ram and rushed headlong over a cliff top. Over two thousand sheep perished; their shepherd tried to stop the stampede and was himself swept along and killed.

This sort of behaviour is typical of crowds. Instead of behaving like sensible individuals, men and women, boys and girls, change when they become part of a large crowd. They do things they would never dream of doing on their own. Can you think of any examples? (Vandalism often depends on gangs; hooliganism at football matches; crowds gathering to stare at accidents often behave in a cruel, heartless manner; sightseeing crowds have prevented rescuers getting through to the victims of an accident.) Cruel dictators are well aware of the power of crowds to make people forget their sense of fairness or pity. They love to mass people together and then work on their weaknesses and fears. Hitler was a past master at this!

Jesus treated people in just the opposite way. Here is more of what he had to say about the good shepherd.

Reading

So Jesus said again, 'I am telling you the truth: I am the gate for the sheep. All others who came before me are thieves and robbers, but the sheep did not listen to them. I am the gate. Whoever comes in by me will be saved; he will come in and go out and find pasture. The thief comes only in order to steal, kill, and destroy. I have come in order that you might have life—life in all its fullness.

'I am the good shepherd, who is willing to die for the sheep. When the hired man, who is not a shepherd and does not own the sheep, sees a wolf coming, he leaves the sheep and runs away; so the wolf snatches the sheep and scatters them. The hired man runs away because he is only a hired man and does not care about the sheep. I am the good shepherd. As the Father knows me and I know the Father, in the same way I know my sheep and they know me. And I am willing to die for them.'

(John 10.7-15, GNB)

Comment

Jesus called himself the gate or door of the sheep. Often at night the sheep were enclosed in roughly made stone or thorn folds. The shepherd slept in the only opening so he *was* the doorway. Any thieves or wild animals would have to get past him. He put his own life at risk for the sheep.

Remember how the shepherd knew all his sheep by name. In another parable, Jesus told how the good shepherd would go off looking for a lost sheep even though he had ninety-nine safely in the fold. Jesus treats us all as separate, unique people. He tells us of God's love for each one, not for crowds. He asks us to follow him, to listen to his voice. But he does not *make* us. We can behave like foolish sheep if we wish.

Prayer

Almighty God, our heavenly Father, we thank you for our lives here and for the freedom we have to choose between right and wrong. When we are faced with temptation, give us strength of mind to do what is right and guide us in our decisions. Forgive us for the many times we have done wrong, led on by selfishness, boastfulness, or by forgetting your teaching. Help us to remember that we too set an example to others. Guide us today and every day as we try to follow in the footsteps of our brave shepherd, Jesus Christ our Lord.

Hymns

Lord, you are my shepherd   (SNS 18)
The Lord's my shepherd, I'll not want
There are hundreds of sparrows   (CP 15)

Music

Handel: *He shall feed his flock* from *The Messiah.*

Follow-up for the class-room

1   Read the parable of the lost sheep in Luke 15.4-7. Remembering that parables teach *one* important truth, discuss what this parable teaches.

2   Talk about the reasons why a bishop carries a crozier, a kind of symbolic crook.

3   Make a model of an eastern sheepfold. Make model sheep, and a shepherd. Put the shepherd in the narrow opening and label your model, 'I am the gate of the sheep'.

4   A number of hymns are based on Psalm 23. Read this psalm. The poet thinks of God as a shepherd. How does he show that God cares for each one of us? Either discuss as a group, or write individual answers.

Words, words, words

It is intended that children shall take the greater part of the Assembly, and some rehearsal may be necessary. Alternatively, the material may be used as a normal Assembly, with the leader taking all the readers' parts.

The Assembly

Preparation
Ask a number of children to each bring a book of a particular kind, and to be ready to show it and say what kind of book it is. Have a table ready so that the books can then be displayed.

Ask a number of children to think about a favourite word and to be prepared to say why it is a favourite. The word could be chosen because of an association or because of its sound.

Learn the song *Every word comes alive* from *Come and Praise* (no 72).

Introduction
The children who have brought books hold them up one at a time, show them to the whole group, and say what kind of book it is. They then add them to the display of books. The books should include, for example, a dictionary, an encyclopaedia, a novel, a science book, a book of plays, a poetry book, the Bible, a cookery book, etc.

Reader 1: In these books are millions of words. There are hard words and easy ones, old ones and new ones. There are words saying what other words mean. There are words that rhyme and make poems. There are words that describe the heavens and others that tell of the wonders of earth. But they are lifeless.

Reader 2: They are lifeless like puppets waiting for someone to pull the strings and make them live. We bring them to life when we speak them, when we sing them, when we read them. We can use them silently in our own minds, or say them aloud for others to hear. They live in the stories we read, in poems we say, in films and plays we watch. They live when we copy them out, use them in puzzles, tell jokes, describe, invent, or when we simply talk with each other.

Song
Every word comes alive   (CP 72)

Poem
The poet Gerard Manley Hopkins loved words. He wrote this poem called *Pied Beauty*. (Pied means of various colours, like a magpie.)

Glory be to God for dappled things—
    For skies of couple-colour as a brinded cow;
        For rose-moles all in stipple upon trout that swim;
Fresh-firecoal chestnut-falls; finches' wings;
    Landscape plotted and pieced—fold, fallow, and plough;
        And all trades, their gear and tackle and trim.

All things counter, original, spare, strange;
    Whatever is fickle, freckled (who knows how?)
        With swift, slow; sweet, sour; adazzle, dim;
He fathers-forth whose beauty is past change:
                Praise him.

Reader 3: Though Gerard Manley Hopkins is dead we can still read and enjoy his words because they have been written down and published in a book. Books help us to preserve the words of men and women down the ages, so that their words still have life for us today.

Talk
The poet's words were very carefully chosen to express what he felt. But words can also be used thoughtlessly. They can be used as weapons to hurt and injure. There is an old rhyme which says:

        Sticks and stones may break my bones
        But words can never hurt me.

Grown-ups often say that when children have been hurt by something said to them. Perhaps they have been called names. Sometimes ignorant and stupid children say cruel things to someone who is handicapped in some way. Then a grown-up may attempt to comfort that person with the old rhyme. But we all know that it is not really true. Words can and do hurt us very much.

But words can also help. Words can show friendship and love. They can cheer us when we are sad. They can bring us joy and entertain us in stories, songs and poems. One of the names of Jesus was 'The Word', and the Bible is often called 'The Word of God'.

Favourite words
The children who have prepared words tell them one at a time, and say why they have chosen that particular word. The words could also be written down and displayed for everyone to see.

Reading
At first, the people of the whole world had only one language and used the same words. As they wandered about in the East, they came to a plain in Babylonia and settled there. They said to one another, 'Come on! Let's make bricks and bake them hard.' So they had bricks to build with and tar to hold them together. They said, 'Now let's build a city with a tower that reaches the sky, so that we can make a name for ourselves and not be scattered all over the earth.'

Then the Lord came down to see the city and tower which those men had built, and he said, 'Now then, these are all one people and they speak one language; this is just the beginning of what they are going to do. Soon they will be able to do anything they want! Let us go down and mix up their language so that they will not understand one another.' So the Lord scattered them all over the earth, and they stopped building the city. The city was called Babylon, because there the Lord mixed up the language of all the people, and from there he scattered them all over the earth.

(Genesis 11.1-9, GNB)

Comment
Originally, this very old story tried to explain why people speak different languages. The writer of Genesis takes the story a stage further to show

74

that when people cannot understand one another there is disunity and they are unable to co-operate. Words can help to bring people together, but they can also divide.

Prayer
Lord, as we think of the many millions of words that will be used today, some carelessly, some spitefully, some helpfully, some kindly, we pray that our words may not be used to hurt anyone. Help us to be thoughtful in what we say to others.

Follow-up for the class-room

1   An attempt has been made to help people to understand each other by creating a new language for everyone to speak as well as their own. This is called Esperanto. Find out how this language has been made. Discuss whether this is a good idea or not.

2   Read John 1.1-5: Jesus is called the Word. Talk about what John says the Word was used for.

3   Some poets have used the fact that we often delight in the sheer sounds of words to write nonsense poems. Read *Jabberwocky* by Lewis Carroll, and some of Edward Lear's *Nonsense Songs*. Write some nonsense verses.

4   Write a poem or piece of prose about colours or sounds.

5   Learn how to use a Thesaurus; it is a useful book for poets, writers and crossword addicts! Let the group take it in turns to look up a word, perhaps starting with 'pied'.

Towards Easter — 1

Note
It is suggested that the two Assemblies included under this heading are taken consecutively.

The Assembly

Preparation
Arrange for a display of spring bulbs and flowers. Have ready a tape or record of *Spring* from *The Four Seasons* (Vivaldi).

Poem
This is part of a poem called *Spring,* by Gerard Manley Hopkins. It describes the rich, new, vigorous life of springtime.

Nothing is so beautiful as Spring—
   When weeds, in wheels, shoot long and lovely and lush;
   Thrush's eggs look little low heavens, and thrush
Through the echoing timber does so rinse and wring
The ear, it strikes like lightnings to hear him sing;
   The glassy peartree leaves and blooms, they brush
   The descending blue; that blue is all in a rush
With richness; the racing lambs too have fair their fling.

Music
Play *Spring* from *The Four Seasons,* by Vivaldi.

Talk
The poem and music make us aware of the new life and joy and colour which spring brings to the world. But not very long ago, in the winter, it seemed as though everything was dead and colourless.

   From time to time each of us feels as though life has lost all its joy. We are worried. The future looks black. We may feel we will never be really happy again. Then, suddenly, the load is lifted, our hearts feel lighter, we feel full of joy. Life is worth living again. Perhaps we have lost a loved pet and only gradually recovered from our sadness and sense of loss. Perhaps we have been ill, and recovered. Perhaps we have been frightened at facing an operation; we wake up in bed to find it is all over. The relief and happiness is tremendous.

Story

William was very worried indeed, although he was determined not to show it. He had known for some time that his mother was quite ill. She looked ill. She was no longer the happy, energetic person he knew, always busy about something. She needed to spend quite a lot of time in bed. William would have been quite glad if she had told him off for coming in with dirty shoes, or for tearing his clothes. But she no longer did; it was as though all her energy had to be used for fighting her illness. William was very sad. It was winter time, too. The short, dark days seemed in keeping with his gloomy, frightened feelings.

One day William's father told him that Mum had to go into hospital for an operation. Dad's face was grim. He did not try to pretend that it was something trivial. 'I'm afraid it's serious, Bill,' he said. 'You've got to be brave and try to help as much as you can.'

William did try. But his heart was heavy. Life seemed to have lost all its fun. He didn't want to play with his friends. 'I can't be bothered,' he told them. 'I don't feel like it.' It even became too much trouble to eat.

Mum went into hospital. For the first two weeks or so William was not allowed to go to see her. Dad told him the news. The operation was over. He would be able to visit her soon. When William did go he was shaken to see how thin and tired she looked. The weeks passed.

Then William heard that Mum was coming home. Dad told him she was going to be all right. The operation was a success: she was going to be well again. Of course it would take time but the worst was over. At first William could not believe it. He thought Dad was simply trying to cheer him up. Dad was quite annoyed. 'I've always told you the truth,' he said, 'and it's true that Mum is going to get better.'

At last William could believe it. It was as though a huge weight had been lifted from his mind. He felt almost too light to walk: he had to run everywhere. His friends were happy because he was so full of joy. His old zest for both food and games came back with a rush. School was good again.

On his way home on Friday he looked forward to Mum coming home. He thought about all the things he would do to help. As he skipped along the road he looked into the trim gardens and saw there the first signs of spring—the tender green shoots of crocuses and daffodils. The low sun made the sky glow gold and red. He felt alive again.

Hymns
Morning has broken   (CP 1)
When the cold earth feels the sunshine   (SNS 42)

Bible story
On Maundy Thursday in Holy Week, the week before Easter, we remember how Jesus had his last meal with his disciples. He told them he was to die and that they were to remember him by sharing the bread, which was his body, and the wine, which was his blood. Jesus had tried to prepare his disciples; he had warned them more than once that he must soon leave them, that he must suffer and die, but that he would return to them on the third day. Only by doing this could he show God's love for the world.

The disciples had not understood. They thought, perhaps, that Jesus was testing them. They felt that this could not happen to their master. Then, in the Garden of Gethsemane, Jesus was arrested. He had been betrayed by one of his own disciples. The rest of the little group fled for their lives. Jesus was left alone in the hands of his enemies. Peter plucked up enough courage to follow Jesus and his captors to the High Priest's house, but there, in the courtyard, his courage failed him and he denied, with curses, that he even knew Jesus.

Jesus was condemned to die by the Roman governor, Pontius Pilate, and the crowd who a week earlier had shouted, 'Hosanna!' as Jesus rode into Jerusalem, now yelled, 'Crucify him!'

Jesus died on the hill outside the city on Good Friday. He was crucified between two thieves. Some of his friends stayed nearby, among them his mother and John the disciple. Perhaps the rest were near but remained well hidden. They were full of fear; perhaps they too would be arrested and executed. Their hopes were gone: they had thought Jesus was a great leader, the Messiah, who would set up God's kingdom on earth. Now he was dead; it was all finished. They might just as well go back to their old jobs and try to forget the whole thing.

Jesus was taken down from the cross and put into the garden tomb of

Joseph of Arimathaea. It was now the Sabbath and nothing more could be done until it was over. The disciples spent the day in deep despair.

Early on Sunday morning Mary Magdalene went to the tomb, carrying spices with which to anoint Jesus' body: it was all she could do. She saw that the circular stone sealing the tomb entrance had been removed. She ran and told Peter and John, thinking that Jesus' body had been taken away. Peter and John ran back. Peter went in and found the cloths which had wrapped Jesus' body lying on one side. John joined him; they did not know what to think, and finally went back to the other disciples.

But Mary stayed near the tomb. She was the first to see Jesus again.

Prayer
Heavenly Father, we thank you for the signs of new life which we see around us each springtime. After the darkness of winter we are happy to see the spring flowers, the trees budding with new life, and to hear the birds singing as they build their nests. New life is all around us. Thank you, Father.

Follow-up for the class-room

1   Make careful drawings or paintings of spring bulbs and other spring flowers. Find out which wild flowers are to be seen now; one of the earliest is the coltsfoot. Find out what is unusual about this plant.

2   Make an Easter garden showing the cave tomb and the large circular stone which ran in a groove across the entrance. Use small pieces of evergreen for trees and bushes. Decide what to put inside the tomb. The three empty crosses could be shown in the background.

3   Prepare a traditional Easter carol, such as *Cheer up, friends and neighbours* or *Now the green blade riseth from the buried grain* or *The world itself keeps Easter Day* (all from *Oxford Book of Carols*), or a modern Easter hymn or carol (from *The Easter Book,* NCEC).

4   Read *Home thoughts from abroad* by Robert Browning: a famous poem which gives a lovely description of the English countryside in spring.

Towards Easter — 2

The Assembly

Preparation
Arrange for a group of dancers to illustrate 'new life' to the music *The Dance of the Hours* by Poncielli. The dancers, curled up tight, represent seeds buried in the ground. Gradually the warming soil stirs life in them. They awaken and begin to grow. Gradually they push towards light and warmth. Soon they are swaying in the breeze and opening out their flowers to the spring sunshine.

Introduction
Many hundreds of years ago a monk called the Venerable Bede described in his history book how Easter was named after an old Saxon goddess called Eostre. The ancient Saxons used to celebrate the coming of spring, when life returned to the fields and woods, with a special festival.

Christians often used old festivals to mark the special festivals of the Christian year, and the death and resurrection of Jesus was celebrated at Easter because it too celebrates the coming of new life.

One of the traditional ways of celebrating Easter is the giving of Easter eggs. It may be that this custom, too, goes back to before the time of Jesus. Eggs remind us of new life. How? (Inside the hard, dead-looking shell, new life is growing, ready to burst out.) For Christians, eggs remind us of the closed tomb into which Jesus' body was put, and from which new life sprang on Easter morning.

Reading
Early on Sunday morning, while it was still dark, Mary Magdalene went to the tomb and saw that the stone had been taken away from the entrance.

Mary stood crying outside the tomb. While she was still crying, she bent over and looked in the tomb and saw two angels there dressed in white, sitting where the body of Jesus had been, one at the head and the other at the feet. 'Woman, why are you crying?' they asked her.

She answered, 'They have taken my Lord away, and I do not know where they have put him!'

Then she turned round and saw Jesus standing there; but she did not know that it was Jesus. 'Woman, why are you crying?' Jesus asked her. 'Who is it that you are looking for?'

She thought he was the gardener, so she said to him, 'If you took him away, sir, tell me where you have put him, and I will go and get him.'

Jesus said to her, 'Mary!'

She turned towards him and said in Hebrew, 'Rabboni!' (This means 'Teacher'.)

'Do not hold on to me,' Jesus told her, 'because I have not yet gone back up to the Father. But go to my brothers and tell them that I am returning to him who is my Father and their Father, my God and their God.'

So Mary Magdalene went and told the disciples that she had seen the Lord and related to them what he had told her.

(John 20.1, 11-18, GNB)

Comment

So Jesus showed he was alive again. It took time for the disciples to undertstand. Several stories about how Jesus came and spoke to them are included in the gospel records. But, on their own, the stories are not enough to make us believe that Jesus really is alive again. But when we put them alongside what happened to the disciples, that is a different matter. The change in the disciples was tremendous.

Once they had been terrified for their own safety, and full of a hopeless feeling. Now they forgot themselves and were full of joy. They were filled with new life. In order to tell the good news of the gospel they were imprisoned, they were beaten, they endured great hardships. Peter, who had once denied that he even knew Jesus, was, like his master, crucified. So, at Easter, we think of how Jesus, by his resurrection, brought new life to his friends. Christians believe that he still does that today.

Easter greeting

In a part of the Church called Eastern Orthodox—and in many other churches round the world—there is a special Easter greeting. Instead of

people saying, 'Good morning', they greet each other like this:
Voice 1: Christ is risen.
Voice 2: He is risen indeed.
Easter is the greatest, the most important festival, of the Christian Church. Without Easter there could be no Church at all.

Invite the children to respond to your words 'Christ is risen' with the phrase 'He is risen indeed'.

Easter carol, prepared by a group following the previous Assembly.

Dance drama, prepared by dance group, of flowers coming to life.

Hymns
From the darkness came light   (CP 29)
It's Easter! It's Easter! Rejoice and be glad   (SNS 41)
When Jesus walked in Galilee   (CP 25)

Prayer
Heavenly Father, at this time we think of the new life which Jesus brought, of the joy which filled his disciples' hearts as they came to know he was still with them. So great was that joy that they had to share it with everyone they met. Help us to understand that Jesus is alive now and can fill our hearts with joy, too.

Follow-up for the class-room

1   Read the gospel stories of the resurrection of Jesus: John 20 and 21.1-22; Luke 24.1-49.

2   Our calendar is divided into the time before Christ (BC) and the time after his birth (AD—Anno Domini, meaning 'the year of our Lord'). Discuss what this tells about the importance of Jesus for mankind. Read Revelation 1.18, and Jesus' last instructions to his disciples in Matthew 28.19-20. How have these instructions been fulfilled?

Doing what we can

The Assembly

Introduction

We sometimes think that if we need help we have to go to very clever people with special training or skills. Of course that is sometimes true: if we are ill we go to see a doctor; if the television goes wrong we call in a television engineer; if our house starts falling down we would do well to call in a good builder.

But these are special problems. Many problems that people have do not need that kind of expert help; but help *is* needed. One organisation which has been set up to offer help is called 'The Samaritans'.

Talk

There are nearly two hundred branches of The Samaritans throughout the United Kingdom. It started in London in 1953 when a clergyman called Chad Varah set up the first office. His idea was so wonderful that since then the organisation has spread to every part of the country.

For twenty-four hours every day, seven days a week, fifty-two weeks a year, volunteers man telephones and wait for people to contact them. Those who do get in touch are usually in deep despair. They are very unhappy, sometimes frightened, usually lonely and desperately worried. They do not know where to turn for help. Some of them feel that they do not want to live any longer. Every year, more than a quarter of a million people contact The Samaritans for the first time.

What sort of people contact them? People of every kind! Some are quite young children; some are old people. Both rich and poor ask for help. Some have good jobs; some are out of work. Some have families; some are quite alone in the world. In one way they are all alike: they all have problems which they cannot face alone. They call by 'phone, they write letters, sometimes they visit one of the centres. But whichever way they choose to get in touch they know from the start that they will be helped.

The Samaritans are quite ordinary men and women. They are not experts although they are trained for the work they do. They are all volunteers and receive no pay. But whatever time they offer to The Samaritans has to be given regularly and faithfully; the time promised to The Samaritans has to come first. The Samaritans say that above all they are good listeners; people who understand how other people feel and want to help them as a friend would. Those who call for help do not even have to give their names. But if they wish, a Samaritan will meet them, listen to their problems and try to help, and go on helping for as long as necessary. It is good to think that there is someone waiting at the end of a 'phone at any time of the day or night.

We can all learn from The Samaritans. We do not have to be very clever or very rich to help people in trouble. Sometimes what is needed most of all is someone who has time to listen. We can all help our friends in that way.

Hymns
A job to do   (SNS 66)
Would you walk by on the other side   (CP 70)

Reading
This story from the Bible is recorded by all four gospel writers: Matthew, Mark, Luke and John, but only John tells us what a young boy did.

It was near the time of Passover, the great Jewish festival. Raising his eyes and seeing a large crowd coming towards him, Jesus said to Philip, 'Where are we to buy bread to feed these people?' Philip replied, 'Twenty pounds would not buy enough bread for every one of them to have a little.' One of his disciples, Andrew, the brother of Simon Peter, said to him, 'There is a boy here who has five barley loaves and two fishes; but what is that among so many?' Jesus said, 'Make the people sit down.' There was plenty of grass there, so the men sat down, about five thousand of them. Then Jesus took the loaves, gave thanks, and distributed them to the people as they sat there. He did the same with the fishes, and they had as much as they wanted. When everyone had had enough, he said to his disciples, 'Collect the pieces left over, so that nothing may be lost.' This they did, and filled twelve baskets with the pieces left uneaten of the five barley loaves.

(John 6.4-5, 7-13, NEB)

The boy had probably been given the loaves and fishes by his mother for a picnic meal. He offered them to Jesus and, little though the gift was, Jesus was able to use it.

This story is really a parable which teaches a wonderful truth. If we offer what we have, however small it may be, Jesus is able to use it. On the other hand, if we offer nothing Jesus is not able to do his work in the world.

Hymns
We are the hands of Christ   (SNS 56)
When I needed a neighbour were you there   (CP 65)

Prayer
Heavenly Father, help us to be like the boy in the story and offer what we can. When those in our family, or our friends, or those we meet, need us to listen to them, or just to be with them, may we not turn away, but give what help we can, gladly and willingly.

Follow-up for the class-room

1   Read Luke 10.29-37. Write down the probable reason why Chad Varah called his organisation The Samaritans.

2   Invite a volunteer from the Citizens' Advice Bureau to talk about its work.

3   Make an exhibition of the work of Christian Aid, a branch of the World Council of Churches. Leaflets and posters may be obtained from the local office of Christian Aid.

4   Many societies have been set up to meet special needs, such as MENCAP for the mentally handicapped, The Spastics Society, The Royal National Institute for the Blind. Find out about the local activities of these and similar organisations. Arrange for children to prepare short talks about their work.

Made like God

The Assembly

Preparation

Obtain a picture of a warship of the Napoleonic period, if possible, and one showing cave paintings, for use during the stories.

Arrange for a group to present a short dance movement they have devised expressing a piece of music.

Introduction

Right at the beginning of the Bible, in Genesis Chapter 1, a Hebrew writer gives us his idea of how God made the world. Of course it is a story. If we were to write a story today about how the world started it would be very different because we know a lot more science than this writer. We would probably talk about the Big Bang Theory—how matter was once concentrated in a very small space and then, following a huge explosion, it spread out into space, eventually forming all the stars and planets. But the Hebrew writer had hold of a very important truth. God created or made the universe and all that is in it. More than that, God was pleased with his creation. Here is part of the story. God has created nearly all the universe and now he decides to make one more creature.

Reading

Then God said, 'And now we will make human beings; they will be like us and resemble us. They will have power over the fish, the birds, and all animals, domestic and wild, large and small.' So God created human beings, making them to be like himself. He created them male and female, blessed them, and said, 'Have many children, so that your descendants will live all over the earth and bring it under their control. I am putting you in charge of the fish, the birds, and all the wild animals. I have provided all kinds of grain and all kinds of fruit for you to eat; but for all the wild animals and for all the birds I have provided grass and leafy plants for food'—and it was done. God looked at everything he had made, and he was very pleased. Evening passed and morning came— that was the sixth day.

And so the whole universe was completed. By the seventh day God finished what he had been doing and stopped working. He blessed the seventh day and set it apart as a special day, because by that day he had completed his creation and stopped working. And that is how the universe was created.

(Genesis 1.26 to 2.4, GNB)

Comment
Did you notice that when God made human beings he said they would be rather special? In what ways were they to be special? He said they would be like himself and they would be in control of the earth.

This story shows one important way in which humans are like God.

Story: The cave paintings of Lascaux
In the summer of 1940 a very important discovery was made at Lascaux in the Dordogne, in Southern France. A new series of caves was found which had not seen the light of day for over 20,000 years. What was so exciting about this discovery was that the walls of the caves were covered with magnificent paintings; there were even paintings on top of paintings. The paintings had been preserved by a sort of calcite glaze, the same sort of mineral that makes stalactites and stalagmites. The paintings showed the wild cattle of the Stone Age. The oldest paintings were perhaps as old as 30,000 years. They also showed deer and horses. The observation of the artists was very acute and the drawings, often done with just a few deft strokes, really bring the animals to life. They are full of movement. *(Display picture of cave paintings)*

One of the prehistoric artists left behind his simple lamp, a hollowed-out stone. There was also a pestle and mortar which had been used to grind up the three colours: ochre, red and black. These were the only colours used.

Scholars who study prehistoric remains, palaeontologists, believe that Lascaux might have been an important centre for religion and magic and that is why it has so many paintings. Perhaps these ancient peoples thought that their paintings would help the hunters to catch the animals they had depicted so beautifully on the cave walls. Perhaps they were making a kind of magic. We do not know and will never know for sure; but one thing is certain: they were really creative artists.

Comment

These ancient people were like God in that they were creators. They made beautiful things which we can look at with pleasure today. They were artists, pleased with what they had created.

Man, like God, is a creator. This is one of the things that marks man out from the other animals. Of course, some animals make things. Can you think of examples? (Birds' nests, spiders' webs, ant hills, wasps' nests, beavers' dams, and others.) In what ways are man's creations different? (Animals construct by instinct; their webs and nests and dens are much alike. Man's creations are infinitely varied. We can copy too, but we do not have to.)

Dance

Here is a dance by a group. It is different from any other dance that has been made up. It is the group's creation. *The group dances.*

Story: Models from bones

The urge in man to create is so strong that it has to find some way of expressing itself. Even when people have had no proper materials to work with, they have still managed to create.

The wars with the French, which followed the Revolution, lasted from 1792 until the great Battle of Waterloo in 1815 when Napoleon was finally defeated. *(Display the picture of a ship from Napoleonic wars.)*

During those years many Frenchmen were taken prisoner, including sailors whose ships were either sunk or captured by the British Navy. Many of the sailors were brought as prisoners of war to this country. Some were put in special camps, some in hulks, which were large ships moored to the land, others in ordinary prisons. The sailors were ordinary men, often unable to read or write. They had little to do and the days and nights must have seemed very long and dreary.

Some began to amuse themselves by making things, as they had done on board ship. They had to use whatever materials they could find.

Bones from their food were plentiful enough. For tools they had only a sharp knife—probably the same knife they used to cut up their food. But they had plenty of time, patience, and quite remarkable skill. They began to carve models of the ships they had sailed in. They did not need plans: they knew every inch of their old boats, whether they were the great ships of the line with their complicated rigging or the smaller frigates and sloops. Perhaps they remembered the small sailing boats they had used for fishing before joining the French Navy. They carved away at the bones, making the main structure of the ship in great detail. They made rigging from threads drawn from scraps of cloth, or even from their own long hair. Metal parts were made from bits of wire. Some splendid models even had parts made from gold and silver taken from coins or ear-rings which many sailors wore. Scraps of wood were made into beautiful boxes. Straw, dyed with natural dyes, was used as a kind of inlay for decoration. Games were made, the pieces beautifully carved and decorated.

Even in the early 19th century many of these pieces were bought from the prisoners by rich visitors who appreciated the skill and artistry of the craftsmen. Today 'prisoner of war work', as it is called, is eagerly collected. Occasionally exhibitions are held and it is wonderful to see the variety of work produced under such difficult conditions and with such unpromising materials. But creativity will always find a way to express itself.

Hymns
Creator God, you formed the earth   (SNS 10)
I will bring to you the best gift I can offer   (CP 59)

Prayer
Lord, you enjoyed making the world.
Thank you for making us creators, too.
  We love to dance.
  We love to paint and to use clay.
  We love to smell the fresh tang of newly sawn wood.
  We love to use sounds to make music.
  We love to use words to create stories and poems.
Help us to use our abilities to create to delight ourselves and those around us.

Follow-up for the class-room

1 Prepare a display and invite other classes to view it. Each child should create something: a painting, a model, a piece of knitting or needlework, a poem or story, a song or tune.

2 Every civilisation has produced its own kind of art. Find out as much as possible about one or more of these: Ancient Egyptian art, Aboriginal art in Australia, American Indian art, Chinese art, early Nigerian art, Celtic art.

3 Great scientists and mathematicians are also creative people. Find out about some of the following and say what each is especially remembered for (in some cases a selection will have to be made as so much was achieved by one person): Isaac Newton, Christopher Wren, Albert Einstein, Michael Faraday, John Dalton, Charles Darwin.

4 Painting is an important art. From time to time an artist sets new, different standards; he sees things in a new way and makes us try to do the same. Look at some pictures by Picasso. How is he different from many artists who went before him? Discuss.

5 Read Psalm 104, a psalm in praise of God the Creator, and learn verse 24.

Conscience

The Assembly

Preparation
Have ready a reel of cotton for the demonstration.

Introduction
Often, when we do something wrong, someone tells us it is wrong. It may be a parent or a friend, but sometimes we tell ourselves. It is almost as though a voice inside us tells us not to do something. What do we call that voice? (Conscience) The dictionary tells us that the word 'conscience' comes from a Latin word *conscire*, which means to know well in one's own mind.

Talk
If you were to ask a number of people if they are honest, they might well be annoyed with you for asking such a question. Most people *are* honest . . . up to a point. They do not steal from shops or other people's houses. They pay their way and do not like to be in debt. But there are some areas of life where they might not be quite so particular. One of these is paying taxes. Many people think they pay far too much in taxes anyway, so if they can get away with a tax dodge they will. Perhaps they work in their spare time and get paid for it; they do not declare that on their tax form. The tax inspector has no way of finding out!

A tax inspector in a radio interview was talking about his job. 'Every now and then,' he said, 'we get a surprise. The other day we received a brown paper parcel with £500 in old £5 notes. Inside was a note which simply said, "This is to settle an old debt." There was nothing to show where it had come from. At the bottom of the note was added, "Please acknowledge receipt in the personal column of *The Guardian*." We often get surprises like that,' he said.

Why do you think people sometimes send money to tax inspectors in that way? Keep your ideas to yourself while you listen to this story.

Story

Do you know the story of Ali Baba's cave? A poor woodman overheard some magic words 'Open Sesame' and used them to get into a cave where forty thieves had stacked all their plunder. He found himself surrounded by wealth beyond his dreams.

This story is about a man who got into a similar place but by very different means. He had spent many years in the army and had been discharged with a very good record. He had been decorated for bravery on more than one occasion and he had always been strictly honest. In civilian life he found it hard to settle down. He could not find a job and debts began to mount up; he got behind with his rent. His wife and family began to suffer too, not only because he could not provide them with enough money for food and clothing but also because he was becoming very moody and bad-tempered. He began to think of himself as a failure although he had been such a good and successful soldier.

One day he was gazing idly in the window of a jeweller's shop. He laughed bitterly to himself when he saw some of the rings and brooches priced at many hundreds of pounds each. Then he noticed that the shop next door was empty, with a TO LET notice on it. He had an idea.

He decided he would use the skills he had learned in the army to rob the jeweller's shop. He had been an engineer and knew what was needed. Eventually he had everything ready. He broke into the empty shop and began the slow, laborious task of breaking through into the jeweller's next door. He had plenty of time and he worked away secure in the knowledge that no one could hear him.

After several hours' hard work he broke into the strong-room of the jeweller's shop. It was just like Ali Baba's cave. There was rack upon rack of precious things: gold, silver, jewels. It was all his for the taking. But he took none of it. He turned and crawled back through the hole and went home empty-handed.

What do you think stopped him from taking what he wanted? It was not the locks, nor the thick walls, nor the burglar alarms, nor fear. It was something else, something inside. It was his conscience.

Hymns

Love's a gift that's good and free   (SNS 46)
My faith, it is an oaken staff

Talk and demonstration

Conscience has been described as something with sharp corners which is inside a person. When we do something mean or cruel or when we are tempted to do those things then conscience begins to move and the sharp corners hurt. Our conscience pricks us.

We can, and often do, ignore the pain or pangs or pricks of conscience. If we do that too often, the sharp corners gradually become blunted and eventually we do not notice conscience at all.

That happens sometimes with things like stealing. It may start with small things. Conscience gives us a twinge but we don't bother. Gradually the thefts become bigger, the twinges get less and less until they disappear altogether. A habit has been formed because we ignored the twinges of conscience and habits like this are hard to break.

This demonstration may help you. *(Ask a child to come forward and hold out his arms; make sure they are well covered by clothing. Take a reel of cotton and wind it round the arms two or three times and tie it. Ask the child to break out from the tied cotton; he should do it easily.)* After once or twice it is easy to break away. *(Repeat the actions, but wind the cotton round about a dozen times. Even a strong child will find it difficult to break out.)*

Reading

Companions sometimes make us do wrong because we are frightened that they will laugh at us or will say things that hurt us if we do not join in the wrongdoing. The reading reminds us that we should not worry about that. It is more important to keep our conscience clear.

Who will harm you if you are eager to do what is good? But even if you should suffer for doing what is right, how happy you are! Do not be afraid of anyone, and do not worry. But have reverence for Christ in your hearts, and honour him as Lord. Be ready at all times to answer anyone who asks you to explain the hope you have in you, but do it with gentleness and respect. Keep your conscience clear, so that when you are insulted, those who speak evil of your good conduct as followers of Christ will be ashamed of what they say.

(1 Peter 3.13-16, GNB)

Hymns
Lord of all hopefulness, Lord of all joy
When we're thinking what to do   (SNS 20)

Prayer
Heavenly Father, at the start of this busy day we come to you for a few moments in prayer. Hear us now as we make our own prayers in silence. You know the special worries we have. *(Silence)*

Guide us this day, Lord, in everything we do. If we are tempted to do wrong, speak to us through our consciences. We pray that we may listen so that they remain sharp and alive.

Follow-up for the class-room

1 Some people say that conscience is simply what is taught to young children about right and wrong. Discuss whether this is true, and whether early training is important. Think of reasons why this is not the whole story.

2 Write a story about someone who had a twinge of conscience, describing the feeling.

3 Read Luke 19.1-9: the story of Zacchaeus. Discuss why he decided to give half his belongings to the poor.

Being sorry

The Assembly

Introduction
There are many times a day when we say, 'I'm sorry.' Invite the children
to give examples. (When we jostle someone by mistake. When we fail to
hear what someone has said. When we forget to do something. When we
are late for an appointment.) We use 'Sorry' so often that it has come to
have very little meaning. We have to use other words *with* 'sorry' to show
what we feel when matters are more serious. We say, 'I'm *really* sorry', or
'I'm *deeply* sorry', or 'I am *desperately* sorry', or 'I am *ever so* sorry'.

Story
Billy was very good at saying sorry. If he dirtied the carpet because he
forgot to wipe his muddy shoes as he came indoors he said, 'Sorry,
Mum!' and promptly did it again the next time he came in. He was sorry
when he tore his coat. It happened three times in one month. He was
sorry when his mother complained about the state of his room, but it was
his room and he liked it that way. It never did change much no matter
how often he said he was sorry about it.

He was sorry when his father complained about the way he treated his
young brother. Billy had forgotten all about him when they were in the
park and he had begun to play football with his friends. He had gone
home without him and he had had to be brought home by old Mrs Green
who lived next door but one. He didn't feel it was his job to look after a
brother who couldn't just stand still and watch him play football. He was
very sorry that he forgot to bring him home from school the very next
day. He was found crying near the junior entrance by one of the teachers
and taken home.

In other words, Billy was becoming thoroughly selfish and thought
that if he just said, 'Sorry', everything was magically all right.

Mum was quite worried about it; Dad said it was only boy-like and that Billy would soon grow out of it. At least, he said that before Billy said 'Sorry' for kicking his football against the side of the car and scratching it. Dad might even have let that pass as simply boyish had not Billy done exactly the same thing to the other side of the car the next day. It was then that Dad quite definitely agreed with Mum that something had to be done about Billy.

They decided to have a 'Sorry' campaign of their own. When Billy went up to bed that night he found it just as he had left it that morning. 'Mum,' he called down, 'my bed's not been made!'

'Sorry, dear,' his mother called back. 'I've not had time today.'

Billy waited, expecting to hear her coming up to make his bed. Nothing happened. Time passed. He made it himself.

He came home from school next day ravenously hungry. He was looking forward to fish fingers and chips, the usual Friday tea. Imagine his disgust when he found it was stew, his least favourite meal. 'Oh, Mum,' he cried, 'where's the fish fingers?'

'Sorry, dear,' she said rather absently, 'I clean forgot. Eat your lovely stew.' To make matters worse, they had stew for three days running, even though he told his mother how much he disliked it. Mum was very sorry about it.

Dad was sorry, too, on Saturday morning when he had no change for Billy's pocket money. Billy said he would take a note and get change. But Dad reminded him of how sorry Billy had been last time he had done that, when he had come back with 20p short. Dad was even sorrier later when he came back from shopping to confess that he still had no change. 'I'll be forgetting my own name next,' he laughed. 'Sorry, I clean forgot. I'll give it to you later.'

Billy had to keep asking till Monday morning, when Dad gave him half of it. Then Dad took that back as well. He reminded Billy of how sorry he had been when he ruined the new paint brush by using it to glue a model. 'This will just about take care of that,' said Dad.

The 'Sorry' campaign went on for a few days more till Billy began to understand. 'You're trying to teach me something,' he announced. 'I think I know what. When you say "Sorry" you've got to do something about it as well as just saying it.'

'Right,' said Mum. 'We're sorry we had to make life just a little unpleasant but we hope it was all worth it.'

And it was. Mum had only to murmur 'stew' and Billy was tidying his room, cleaning his shoes, and generally behaving quite well. He had learned that if you really mean you are sorry, you have to *feel* something inside, and try to do something about it.

Reading

It is one of the marks of a great man that he is able to say he is sorry to someone who is far below him in rank. It is also true that the higher up a person is, the harder it is for him to realise that he needs to feel sorry about something. A long time ago, kings were often thought of as being right whatever they did. This was not true in Israel. There were always men of God, prophets, who were quite ready to tell even kings that they had done wrong and should be ashamed of their actions.

Probably the greatest king Israel ever had was King David. Later he was thought of as the ideal king. Yet David was far from perfect. Once he fell in love with a woman called Bathsheba, who was already married. Her husband was a soldier called Uriah. He was not a Jew but a kind of mercenary soldier who fought for the Jews in return for pay. David determined to have Bathsheba as his wife. To get rid of Uriah he had him sent to the fiercest part of the battle line knowing that he would be killed, as indeed he was. Then David married Bathsheba.

But there was a prophet called Nathan who learned what David had done and he decided, king or not, to confront him with his terrible deed.

The Lord sent the prophet Nathan to David. Nathan went to him and said, 'There were two men who lived in the same town; one was rich and the other poor. The rich man had many cattle and sheep, while the poor man had only one lamb, which he had bought. He took care of it, and it grew up in his home with his children. He would feed it with some of his own food, let it drink from his cup, and hold it in his lap. The lamb was like a daughter to him. One day a visitor arrived at the rich man's home. The rich man didn't want to kill one of his own animals to prepare a meal for him; instead, he took the poor man's lamb and cooked a meal for his guest.'

David was very angry with the rich man and said, 'I swear by the living Lord that the man who did this ought to die! For having done such a cruel thing, he must pay back four times as much as he took.'

'You are that man,' Nathan said to David. 'You had Uriah killed in battle; and then you took his wife!'

'I have sinned against the Lord,' David said.

(2 Samuel 12.1-7a, part of 9, 13a, GNB)

Hymns
Heavenly Father, may thy blessing   (CP 62)
I've heard of one called Jesus   (SNS 32)

Prayer
Lord, we often do wrong things because we are thoughtless. Sometimes we do them because we are frightened of what others may say or do. Help us to understand what it means to be sorry. Show us how to overcome our weakness and selfishness and so to know that we are forgiven.

Follow-up for the class-room

1   Use a dictionary to find the derivation of the word 'sorry'. Note that it is not related to 'sorrow', but to 'sore'.

2   King David had not really taken a poor man's pet lamb to make a meal for a visitor. Write down the reasons why Nathan told this story. How do we know that David was sorry for his action?

3   Read the story Jesus told in Luke 15.11-24. Find out what happened after the son who went away came back and said he was sorry for what he had done. Discuss what this tells us about the way God treats us.

The importance of forgiving

The Assembly

Preparation
A teacher and two children should rehearse the drama.

Introduction
Ask the children if they know what a feud is. (One dictionary says it is lasting mutual hostility, that is hostility on both sides, between two tribes, families or people, with murderous assaults in revenge for previous injury.) In this scene we see how children can sometimes start a kind of feud even though the assaults may not be exactly murderous.

Drama
Two girls are fighting. A teacher approaches and parts them. They continue to glare at each other.
Teacher: And what was all that about?
Tracey: It's her. She's always getting me into trouble.
Teacher: What did she do?
Tracey: She pushed me against the shelf and all the books crashed down. I gave her a dig and she started crying. Then Miss came in and said it was my fault.
Teacher: What have you to say, Christine?
Christine: That's just like her. She's always trying to cause trouble. She gets her friends on to me at playtime. And it wasn't a dig, it was a thump.
Teacher: Did she do that this playtime?
Christine: Yes. They all stood round making fun of me and calling me 'Williams' and things.
Teacher: But your name is Williams.
Christine: It's the way they say it, with a kind of sneer.
Tracey: That's because her friends waited for me outside school last night

99

and took my coat and threw it in a puddle.

Teacher: It sounds to me as if this has been going on for a long time.

Tracey: It has. It started about two years ago.

Christine: I didn't like her in the Infants.

Teacher: Good heavens! All that time ago! How did it start? *(Tracey and Christine are both silent.)* Well?

Tracey: I can't remember.

Teacher: Can you remember, Christine?

Christine: Well . . . no.

Talk and Story

Because of a small incident a long time ago, Tracey and Christine both harboured grudges, refusing to forgive each other. A nasty feud developed; others became involved. Now they cannot even remember how it all started. This is how more serious feuds develop, as this famous story shows.

Does anyone know the title of what is probably the most famous love story in the world? *(Romeo and Juliet)* Shakespeare turned the story into a play although he did not himself make up the story. The play is a tragedy because it has an unhappy ending and that unhappy ending was the result of a feud between the two families to which Romeo and Juliet belonged.

The Montagues and Capulets were amongst the chief families of Verona in Italy. But for longer than anyone could remember there had been a bitter feud between them. If members of the two families met in the streets there was sure to be a fight. People on both sides had been killed.

Romeo, who was the son of Lord Montague, attended a feast given by Lord Capulet. He went in disguise, otherwise he would have been dealt with very quickly. Whilst there he saw Juliet, the daughter of Lord Capulet. They fell in love with each other. There was no hope that they would be allowed to marry openly, so they agreed to marry in secret. The wedding took place the next day with the help of Friar Laurence. The good friar intended to tell about the marriage at a suitable moment.

Alas, Romeo was caught up in a street fight with his enemies and the Prince, who ruled the city, banished him to Mantua as a punishment. Juliet was very sad and pined for Romeo. Her father, Lord Capulet, thought it was time she married and suggested Count Paris who was a kinsman. Juliet made excuses but in the end her father insisted. She went for advice to Friar Laurence who told her to agree to the marriage; but before it could take place she must drink a potion. This would do her no real harm, but it would make her unconscious and it would look as though she was dead. The effect of the drug would last only forty hours. The friar promised to warn Romeo of what she had done. Romeo would come to rescue her from the vault where she would be lying and carry her to Mantua and safety.

But things went badly wrong. Romeo did not get the friar's message. Instead he heard that Juliet was dead. He bought a poison, and came to the vault where Juliet lay. Outside the vault he met Count Paris. They drew their swords. Paris was killed. Romeo went into the vault to see Juliet for the last time. He gave her a parting kiss, then took the poison and died. Juliet wakened up and found him. She guessed what had happened and she stabbed herself through the heart and died.

So the tragic story ended. Because of the evil that grew and flourished through the years, through a refusal to forgive, two innocent members of the feuding families died. Evil feeds and grows like a disease. The only thing that can stop it is a willingness to forgive.

When the heads of the Montague and Capulet families saw what had happened they realised what their senseless feud had done. At last they were reconciled to each other. But it was too late for Romeo and Juliet.

Reading

The idea of forgiveness is one of the most important in the gospel. After Jesus had taught his disciples to pray, he said:

'If you forgive others the wrongs they have done to you, your Father in heaven will also forgive you. But if you do not forgive others, then your Father will not forgive the wrongs you have done.'

(Matthew 6.14-15, GNB)

On another occasion:

Peter came to Jesus and asked, 'Lord, if my brother keeps on sinning against me, how many times do I have to forgive him? Seven times?'

'No, not seven times,' answered Jesus, 'but seventy times seven, because the Kingdom of heaven is like this. Once there was a king who decided to check on his servants' accounts. He had just begun to do so when one of them was brought in who owed him millions of pounds. The servant did not have enough to pay his debt, so the king ordered him to be sold as a slave, with his wife and his children and all that he had, in order to pay the debt. The servant fell on his knees before the king. "Be patient with me," he begged, "and I will pay you everything!" The king felt sorry for him, so he forgave him the debt and let him go.

'Then the man went out and met one of his fellow-servants who owed him a few pounds. He grabbed him and started choking him. "Pay back what you owe me!" he said. His fellow-servant fell down and begged him, "Be patient with me, and I will pay you back!" But he refused; instead, he had him thrown into jail until he should pay the debt. When the other servants saw what had happened, they were very upset and went to the king and told him everything. So he called the servant in. "You worthless slave!" he said. "I forgave you the whole amount you owed me, just because you asked me to. You should have had mercy on your fellow-servant, just as I had mercy on you." The king was very angry, and he sent the servant to jail to be punished until he should pay back the whole amount.'

And Jesus concluded, 'That is how my Father in heaven will treat every one of you unless you forgive your brother from your heart.'

(Matthew 18.21-35, GNB)

Hymns
Jesus came teaching   (SNS 33)
When Jesus walked in Galilee   (CP 25)

Prayer
Lord, you have taught us that if we wish to be forgiven then we must also forgive. Help us to forgive the wrong things that are done to us. Help us to be peacemakers. Sometimes it is very hard to forgive, because we feel that others may think we are afraid or weak, but you have taught us that without forgiveness there can be no happiness or joy or peace.

The Lord's Prayer

Follow-up for the class-room

1   Ask the children to write down in their own words what they think Jesus meant by telling Peter that he must forgive 'seventy times seven'.

2   Read how Jesus put his own teaching into practice, in Luke 23.32-34.

3   The story of the unforgiving servant found in Matthew 18.21-35 is very dramatic. Make it into a play. Many of the speeches are already written but some will need to be added.

4   'Forgive' comes from the Anglo-Saxon word *forgiefan* which means 'to give away'. Discuss what this adds to our understanding of what it means to forgive.

Being responsible

The Assembly

Preparation
Select a recorded piece of music with plenty of orchestral colour such as the opening of *Pastoral Symphony* (Beethoven) or the theme and first few variations of *The Young Person's Guide to the Orchestra* (Britten).

Music as selected (see Preparation).

Reading
The reading is part of a well-known passage from Paul's first letter to the Corinthians. In the church at Corinth there had been bad feeling between people. Paul was concerned to show his readers that there is no place for this kind of thing in the church which is called Christ's body. In the church, as in the body, every part is different and each has its part to play.

For the body itself is not made up of only one part, but of many parts. If the foot were to say, 'Because I am not a hand, I don't belong to the body,' that would not keep it from being a part of the body. And if the ear were to say, 'Because I am not an eye, I don't belong to the body,' that would not keep it from being a part of the body. If the whole body were just an eye, how could it hear? And if it were only an ear, how could it smell? As it is, however, God put every different part in the body just as he wanted it to be. There would not be a body if it were all only one part! As it is, there are many parts but one body.

(1 Corinthians 12.14-20, GNB)

Comment
What Paul wrote about the church being like a body is also true of a family and a school. We all listened to the piece of music which started

104

our assembly so beautifully. The sound was made up of contributions from a lot of different instruments, some very large such as the string bass, some very small such as the piccolo. Some of the instruments are struck, some are blown, some are bowed or plucked. They all have a part to play and without their part the whole sound would be poorer.

Each member has a part to play. Some play bigger parts than others but no one can play *your* part except you, and how you play your part helps to decide what the whole school, or family, or church is like.

Talk

In one of Jesus' stories he told how a rich man gave three of his servants different amounts of money to trade with while he was away. To one he gave five thousand silver coins, to another two thousand and to the third one thousand. He decided how much each man could handle. When he came back he asked each what profit he had made. The two who received most did well and were praised. The one who received least had made no profit: he had simply buried the money and returned exactly what he had been given. His master was very angry and took the money from him and gave it to the one who had the most.

In this story, Jesus is showing that we have all been given abilities and so we are all expected to play our part. That part may not always seem very important or glamorous.

Story: Care in small things

Tom Johnson was soon to leave school. He was sixteen and happy to be leaving because he had a good job to go to. Tom was first class at woodwork and he wanted to be a cabinet-maker: a top job in woodworking. His father had a friend, Frank Cox, who was owner and manager of a small firm of cabinet-makers. Tom's father had proudly shown his friend some of the things Tom had made at school. They included a coffee table and a small bookcase. Frank Cox had been impressed. The small pieces were soundly made and beautifully finished. He would give Tom a six-month trial period in the workshop and, if he proved suitable, an apprenticeship. Tom would be taught everything about the trade and eventually would become a fully-fledged cabinet-maker.

Tom reported for work and Frank Cox showed him round the workshop introducing him to the men and boys working there. Tom was thrilled by what he saw. On the benches and in the store-room he saw the most exquisite work, lovely tables, carved sideboards, inlaid desks and cabinets. He couldn't wait to get started. But he had to wait. That day he was taught how to make a good cup of tea. He ran errands to get lunches. He swept up the wood shavings and sawdust. He helped to move things. He did not even touch a saw or a chisel.

Three weeks passed and Tom found himself still doing the same things. True, he had been shown how to sharpen chisels and he was learning the difficult art of setting a saw. But apart from that it was making tea, getting lunches, sweeping, humping, holding. The only sawing he did was to cut logs for the wood stove. But he did it. He did not grumble and he made a good job of whatever he was asked to do.

Another three weeks passed and Tom was getting worried. The routine was just the same. The other two lads, both apprentices, were friendly but said nothing when Tom groused about being a sort of skivvy. Tom's parents suffered at home too. To be honest, they were getting a little worried themselves. Perhaps they had made a mistake. They talked it over and agreed that Tom's father should have a quiet word with his friend Frank Cox and see what was happening. Meanwhile Tom went on with the same old round. When he asked his father if he had spoken to the manager, Dad just grunted and said nothing. 'Much more of this,' thought Tom, 'and I'll be packing it up.'

Six months went by: the end of the trial period. Frank Cox called Tom over. 'Well, Tom,' he said, 'it's time we decided about your apprenticeship. Come with me, we're going on a visit.'

They went in Frank's car to a church some miles away. The firm had been restoring some of the beautiful old furnishings. In the choir above the stalls were some carvings that Frank himself had been working on. He turned on a small floodlight and lit up a carving. 'Just finished this,' he said, 'soon it'll be fixed safely in position.' He handed it to Tom who examined it carefully. It was a carving of an old musician playing a trumpet. The original had been beyond repair and Frank had made a new one; it was perfect. Tom turned it round: it was just as perfect at the back as at the front.

'What a pity people will only be able to see the front when it's fixed in position,' said Tom.

'True,' said Frank, 'but I know what the back's like and so do you. That's the kind of work we do. It's got to be right through and through, not just the bits you can see.'

Later that day Frank Cox called Tom into his office. 'The apprenticeship is yours if you want it. I'll come and see your father.'

'But how can you tell I'm the sort of workman you want?' asked Tom. 'I've not even made a pair of book-ends here!'

'No,' said Frank. 'But I already knew you could work with wood. What I didn't know was whether you were the sort of lad I could rely on no matter what the job was. Sweeping up, sharpening tools, fetching and carrying may not be glamorous or even very important, but they tell me a lot. Remember that carving. I want to be able to trust my men. I think I can trust you.'

Hymns
A job to do   (SNS 66)
He gave me eyes so I could see   (CP 18)
Praise the Lord in the rhythm of your music   (CP 33)

Prayer
Heavenly Father, we are glad that we belong in families and in groups where we each have a part to play. Help us to understand that no one else can play our part. Help us to value everyone in our family and in our school, not just the ones who can do the most or seem the most interesting, but everyone.

Follow-up for the class-room

1   Ask each child to write in his own words why he thinks Frank Cox treated Tom in the way he did when he first joined the workshop.

2   Read the parable of the talents, the story Jesus told, in Matthew 25.14-28, using a modern version.

3   If a ship in the Royal Navy is involved in an accident the captain of the ship is always court-martialled even though the accident may have been the fault of a member of his crew. Discuss why this happens; do members of the group think this is fair?

4   Look up in a dictionary the meaning of 'responsible'. Each child writes about the things for which he is responsible at home. Does he consider himself a responsible person?

Being big headed

The Assembly

Introduction
Invite the children to say what we mean when we call someone big headed. (It is a slang expression for being boastful.) Most of us do not like people who are big headed and we enjoy seeing them brought down a peg or two!

But very boastful people are often in need of help. They need someone who thinks enough of them to tell them the truth. If the big headed person is important this seldom happens. About fifty years ago some of the biggest heads of all time were Hollywood film magnates. They were immensely rich. They decided what would make a good film and they employed some people whose job was to agree with everything they said: they were called 'Yes-men'. If the film magnate had an idea they had to tell him that it was a marvellous idea, a wonderful idea, a certain success. It would have taken a very brave man to tell the truth. As a result, many terrible films were made. You can see some of these awful films when they are repeated on television!

In the Bible there is a story about a very important man who, fortunately for him, had some servants who were willing to tell him the truth.

Story
Long ago, about eight hundred years before Jesus lived, there was a Syrian army commander who had won many victories for his king. Syria was a country bordering on Israel, and the two countries were often at war with each other. But the Syrian commander, Naaman, had leprosy, a dreaded skin disease.

In his household there was a young servant girl, an Israelite who had been captured in one of the many border raids. She had grown fond of her master. One day she told her mistress, Naaman's wife, that there was a man of God in Samaria, in Israel, who could cure Naaman.

Naaman was willing to try anything to be cured. He asked the king of Syria for permission to go to Israel. The king agreed and even wrote a letter to the king of Israel introducing Naaman and asking that he should be cured. Naaman set off taking rich gifts with him.

When the king of Israel received the letter he was petrified. He thought the Syrian king was asking *him* to cure Naaman! 'Does he think that I am God, with the power of life and death?' he demanded. He thought it was a trick, an excuse to start another war.

The prophet Elisha heard what had happened. He told the king to send Naaman to him. Off went Naaman in his chariot, accompanied by his retinue of servants, to Elisha's house. But Elisha did not even come out to see his important visitor. He sent his servant with a message that the commander was to go and wash seven times in the nearby River Jordan. He would then be cured.

Naaman was furious. 'The prophet hasn't even come out,' he said. 'He ought, at least, to have said some prayers and waved his hand over the diseased spot. In any case,' he went on, growing more angry with every minute, 'our rivers in Syria are better than this muddy stream. I could have washed in them and been cured!'

He was going to set off home, highly indignant at having wasted so much time and energy for nothing, but his servants argued with him. 'Sir, if the prophet had told you to do something difficult you would have done it. But because he has told you to do something simple you refuse to do it!'

Naaman's servants were brave to talk to their master like that. They must have felt that he was being foolishly conceited.

Naaman was wise enough to stop and think and take their advice. He went down to the River Jordan. He washed seven times as he had been told—and he was cured. No sign of his disease remained.

A great burden had been lifted from him. He would have done anything for Elisha at that moment. Back he went to the prophet and offered the precious gifts he had brought, as a reward. But Elisha refused to take anything. After all, it was not really the prophet who had cured Naaman, but God. Naaman himself realised this and instead asked Elisha to give *him* a gift. 'Give me two mule-loads of your soil,' he said. 'I will worship the God of Israel in future and this earth will be a constant reminder to me of his dealings with me.'

'Go in peace,' said Elisha.

(From 2 Kings 5.1-19)

Reading

Do we sometimes fail to do things we ought to do because we think they are not important enough for us?

Jesus told a story about someone who thought too much of himself. The Pharisees were religious people who were very particular about keeping every little detail of the Law. In the eyes of most people they were *good* people. Tax collectors, on the other hand, were thought of as wicked people who were not only working for a foreign power but were also lining their own pockets at the expense of quite poor people.

Jesus also told this parable to people who were sure of their own goodness and despised everybody else. 'Once there were two men who went up to the Temple to pray: one was a Pharisee, the other a tax collector.

'The Pharisee stood apart by himself and prayed, "I thank you, God, that I am not greedy, dishonest, or an adulterer, like everybody else. I thank you that I am not like that tax collector over there. I fast two days a week, and I give you a tenth of all my income."

'But the tax collector stood at a distance and would not even raise his face to heaven, but beat on his breast and said, "God have pity on me, a sinner!" I tell you,' said Jesus, 'the tax collector, and not the Pharisee, was in the right with God when he went home. For everyone who makes himself great will be humbled, and everyone who humbles himself will be made great.'

(Luke 18.9-14, GNB)

Comment

Boastful, big headed people are those who forget that their gifts, or their good fortune, has little to do with their own efforts. Instead of feeling grateful they begin to think of how clever they are.

Hymns

Love's a gift that's good and free   (SNS 46)
Thank you, Lord, for this new day   (CP 32)

Prayer

Thank you, Lord, for all your gifts to us. We thank you that we can enjoy so many things. We thank you for minds which we can use to learn. We thank you for the chances you give us every day to help others. May we use our gifts well, Lord, and take those opportunities to help. Stop us from being boastful or conceited. Let us try always to put others' needs before our own.

Follow-up for the class-room

1   Make a short play from the parable of the Pharisee and the tax collector (Luke 18.9-14). The words need little change. Use a narrator to set the scene and to sum up at the end, as Jesus did. Think especially of how the two main characters would show their attitudes by their bearing.

2   Ask each child to write a thumb-nail autobiography saying what his/her strengths and weaknesses are.

3   Write down why big headed people are usually so much disliked.

4   For older groups: Read *Ozymandias* by Percy Bysshe Shelley. This poem says something about having too big an opinion of yourself, even if you are a king.

Sports Day

The Assembly

Preparation
Make large illustrations of the Olympic Games symbol, the Olympic torch, and the Olympic motto (see Talk).

Talk
Ask if anyone can identify the symbol *(show it)*. It is the symbol of the modern Olympic Games. Ask if anyone knows when and how the ancient Games started. (They began in Greece over 700 years BC.) The Games were held every four years at Olympia in honour of Zeus, the king of the gods. The festival went on for five days and was divided into two parts. The first part consisted of offerings to the gods and especially to Zeus. The second part was for athletic contests. At first this was just running; later came the pentathlon, which consisted of five events: leaping, running, throwing the discus, wrestling and throwing the javelin. Later still, boxing was added, and long chariot races were held. Some of the events seem very odd to us, such as racing in armour and races in which the rider jumped off and ran beside his horse. The athletes did not compete for prizes which were valuable in terms of money. The winners received a crown of wild olive leaves. But the important thing was to take part and do your best. Not everyone could join in: only Greeks and Romans were allowed to enter, and there were no women's events. It is from the Greeks that the idea of having great sporting contests came.

The ancient Olympics were abolished in AD 394. Towards the middle of the nineteenth century interest was revived, and it was a Frenchman, Baron Pierre de Coubertin, who had the idea of their becoming an international event. The first modern games took place in Athens in 1896 and like the old games were held every four years. Some of the old contests are still used, but now all kinds of other sports are included, such as cycling, rowing, weight lifting. One main difference between the old and the new Olympics is that women can now take part, and the Games are open to competitors from most countries in the world.

Can anyone say what the torch is used for? *(Show symbol)* An Olympic flame is lit at every Games. The torch is carried by relay runners all the way from Olympia in Greece to light the flame where the Games are to be held. The flame burns throughout the event and represents the spirit of the Games.

The spirit of the Games is represented in another way, too. This is the motto which Baron de Coubertin wrote:

> The important thing in the Olympic Games is not winning but taking part.
> The essential thing in life is not conquering but fighting well.

We all like to win, and sports would not be the same if we did not try to win. But winning is not the most important thing. *How* we win or how we lose matters most. When we win, can we remember those who have lost? When we lose, can we remember to be generous to the winner? A few words make all the difference.

When we have our own sports it will help to remember the Olympic Games motto. *(Say it all together.)*

Readings

In one of Paul's letters to the Corinthian Church he wrote about racing contests and boxing! Probably some of his readers had seen games of this kind because Corinth is in Greece, not too far from Olympia. Paul was really thinking of life as a kind of race.

> Surely you know that many runners take part in a race, but only one of them wins the prize. Every athlete in training submits to strict discipline, in order to be crowned with a wreath that will not last; but we do it for one that will last for ever. That is why I run straight for the finishing-line; that is why I am like a boxer who does not waste his punches. I harden my body with blows and bring it under complete control, to keep myself from being disqualified after having called others to the contest.

(Part of 1 Corinthians 9.24-27, GNB)

Paul is telling us that to be a good follower of Jesus takes many of the qualities of a good athlete. You have to work at it; struggle with the difficulties you meet each day. It is one of the hardest things possible to be a good follower of Jesus. Being a good winner or a good loser is all part of the training of a Christian because he or she thinks of the feelings of others and puts himself or herself last.

Right at the end of his life Paul wrote these words:

The time is here for me to leave this life. I have done my best in the race, I have run the full distance, and I have kept the faith.

(2 Timothy 4.6b-7, GNB)

Hymns
For the excitement of the race   (SNS 71)
The journey of life   (CP 45)

Prayer
Heavenly Father, thank you for games and sports. You know that we all enjoy the thrill of winning. If we are winners, help us to be good winners. If we are losers, help us to be good losers. Help us to remember the feelings of others so that we enjoy not only the racing and the contests but also the sheer fun of taking part. We pray that we may be able to say with Paul, 'I have done my best'.

Follow-up for the class-room

1   Make a copy of the Games symbol; find out what it means and write about it.

2   Find out about the Paraplegic Games. Paraplegics have to overcome a great deal in order to compete or even to live their ordinary lives. What has this to teach those of us who are not handicapped?

3   Discuss why there are so many different events in the Olympic Games. Remember that those taking part are all athletes even though

their skills are very different. Think out how this is a kind of parable. Discuss what this can teach us about the way we should try to develop our skills in ordinary life.

4   Read Aesop's fable called *The Hare and the Tortoise*. Fables have a moral. Was the hare a good athlete? Was the tortoise a good athlete? How did the tortoise manage to win? What is Aesop trying to teach us?

5   Think about this additional story.

Pheidippides was a great runner of ancient Greece. In 490 BC he was sent from Athens to Sparta to tell them about the Persian invasion and to get the warlike Spartans to come and help. He covered the distance of about one hundred and fifty miles very quickly, reaching Sparta on the second day. (Even the best long distance runners of today would find it difficult to equal this feat.)

The Persians met the Greeks in battle at a place called Marathon, a plain on the coast about twenty-six miles from Athens. One hundred and ninety-two Athenians died and their common grave is still to be seen today. After the battle, Pheidippides set out to run the twenty-six miles to Athens to bring them the great news of victory. But he pushed himself so hard that on arrival in the city he collapsed and died. The Marathon race in the modern Olympics is based on Pheidippides' run of twenty-six miles.

Nowadays there is a great revival of interest in marathon running. Sometimes thousands take part, as in the marathons run in London and other big cities. They are certainly run in the true Olympic spirit. Most of the competitors hope only to finish the race and perhaps do a little better than they did the previous time.

Prayer — 1

The Assembly

Preparation
If the children do not already know the Caribbean version of the Lord's Prayer (CP 51), teach it to them. Prepare a group to say the Lord's Prayer in three sections. Select a reader for the modern version of the Lord's Prayer.

Introduction
One day Jesus' disciples came to him and asked him to teach them how to pray. This may seem odd because they were grown men and they had been saying their prayers for a long time. But they had noticed that prayer meant something special to Jesus.

The Lord's Prayer
Probably all of us can say the Lord's Prayer. We have known it for a long time. But it is easy to repeat things we might not really understand. This is the prayer that Jesus taught his disciples in answer to their question. Whole books have been written about this prayer but today we shall think about just three aspects of it.

Group says prayer from 'Our Father . . .' to ' . . . as it is in heaven'.
    The prayer starts by praising God and then goes on to pray that God's will, not ours, should be done on earth. God does not force us to obey. He waits for us to turn to him.

Group says prayer from 'Give us this day . . .' to ' . . . against us'.
    We pray for food but only enough for the day. Jesus knew that greedy people often had so much that others had to go without. Then we pray that our sins—the things we have done wrong—may be forgiven. But Jesus reminds us that this can only happen if *we* forgive others who have

wronged us.

Group says prayer from 'Lead us not into . . .' to the end.

This is the hardest part. We ask that we will not be tested too hard. Remember that Jesus asked God to spare him the pain and suffering of the cross. So Jesus knows what it feels like to be worried about the future. The prayer ends by reminding us that it is God's world, just as in the Garden of Gethsemane Jesus finished his prayer by saying to God, 'Not my will, but your will be done.'

Sing the Lord's Prayer to the Caribbean setting.

Reader
Here is a modern version of the Lord's Prayer:

Our Father,
you alone are God,
may everyone acknowledge and obey you;
may you be obeyed on earth
as you are in heaven.
Give us our food for today.
Forgive us the wrong we have done
as we forgive those who have wronged us.
May we not be tested beyond our strength
and save us from evil.
For the kingdom, the power and the glory
are yours for ever. Amen.

Hymns
Father, hear the prayer we offer
Gladly we pray   (SNS 1)

Talk and prayer
Prayer is speaking and listening. We often think of prayer as a one-way phone line to God—we do all the talking. Prayer should be a conversation with God. We tell him what is in our mind and we listen to see what he has to say to us.

117

When we pray we should first of all thank God for his goodness. Think of things that you have enjoyed. Think of things that have been done for you. Let us do that, silently, now. *(Spend a few moments in silent prayer.)*

Then we should pray for others. Think of actual people who need help: maybe you know of someone who is ill or worried. We will do that now. *(Silence.)*

Last of all we pray for ourselves. We will do that now. *(Silence.)*

God, make us grateful for all that you are to us; sorry for all those things in our lives that hurt your love for us; thankful for all your gifts of life and nature; and ready to serve others in the name of Jesus Christ. Amen.

We do not have to be in church or assembly to pray. But we do have to make time to pray. Jesus spent a lot of time in prayer. Once he spent all night on a hilltop praying to God before he chose his twelve apostles. A good deal of this time would have been spent in thinking and listening. This reminds us that Jesus went into the desert to prepare himself for his work. During that time he prayed and thought and listened. During the three years that Jesus spent teaching and preaching he often went aside quietly to pray. If Jesus needed to do that, how much more do we need to.

Follow-up for the class-room

1   Write prayers of thanksgiving, intercession and petition.

2   Prayers do not need to be long. Some of the finest prayers ever written are short and use simple language. The collects in the Anglican Prayer Book or Alternative Service Book are like this. Find and read some of these. Choose one or two to copy out and learn.

3   Read Luke 11.1-4 in a modern version of the Bible. Compare the words of the prayer with those commonly used. The doxology is not included; but it was probably used from earliest times. Some of the manuscripts of Matthew's gospel include it, or one similar to it. Discuss why this was added, and what it means.

Prayer — 2

The Assembly

Introduction
In our first Assembly on Prayer we realised that prayer is not one-way—us talking to God all the time—but a conversation with God : speaking and listening. Some people give up praying because they do not get what they want right away. They expect an immediate answer. Jesus told a story about that.

Reading
Then Jesus told his disciples a parable to teach them that they should always pray and never become discouraged. 'In a certain town there was a judge who neither feared God nor respected man. And there was a widow in that same town who kept coming to him and pleading for her rights, saying, "Help me against my opponent!" For a long time the judge refused to act, but at last he said to himself, "Even though I don't fear God or respect man, yet because of all the trouble this widow is giving me, I will see to it that she gets her rights. If I don't, she will keep on coming and finally wear me out!" '

   And the Lord continued, 'Listen to what that corrupt judge said. Now will not God judge in favour of his own people who cry to him day and night for help?'

(Luke 18.1-7, GNB)

Comment
Jesus is not saying that God is like that terrible judge who only did something for the poor widow because he was tired of being pestered. Jesus is saying that if such a wicked, careless judge can be *made* to listen, *how much more* will God listen to our prayers.

God *wants* to help us. He *wants* to listen. But sometimes God's answer is 'no' or 'not yet'. It may not be the answer we like or want to hear; but it is an answer just the same.

Story

Mike was fourteen years old. He was fascinated by powerful motor cycles. His father was well off. He was a farmer with a lot of land. He loved his son very much. Mike couldn't wait until he was old enough to have a driving licence. He pestered his father morning, noon and night for a motor bike of his own. 'If only I could have the 1000cc bike, I'd only ride it on the farm. I wouldn't use full power, I promise,' he said.

Mike's father was doubtful: he knew his son could be reckless and impatient at times. He tried to make Mike wait. He knew he should be firm about it, but the pestering went on.

In the end Mike got the powerful machine. His father could not refuse him any longer. At first Mike kept his promise: he only used a fraction of the power and kept on the farm land. But before long he was secretly taking the bike on the unrestricted main road that ran by the farm. One day he went too fast. He lost control. He was thrown off the bike and ended by the side of the road more dead than alive. He was very badly injured. After months in hospital he returned home in a wheelchair. Mike would never ride again.

Talk

Sometimes we say prayers that we do not really mean. Once Jesus saw a man lying by the side of a pool in Jerusalem. He asked the man, 'Do you want to get well?' That seems a strange question because the man was crippled and had been waiting for thirty-eight years for someone to help him. But we can be fooled by appearances.

In a certain town in Italy, in the time of St Francis, there were a number of cripples who used to sit against the wall of a church where, it was said, miracles of healing had taken place. Each cripple had a prayer above his head which said, 'O St Martin, heal me!' In front of each man was a begging bowl into which passers-by dropped coins.

One day the beggars heard the rumour that St Francis was to pass that way. It was believed that he could heal the sick and crippled. No sooner had the word been passed round than the beggars grabbed their prayer cards and their begging bowls and hobbled off as fast as they could.

Healing would have taken away their living!
Be sure when you pray that you really want what you ask for.

Hymns
Praise God, all living things   (SNS 7)
Sad, puzzled eyes of small, hungry children   (SNS 80)

Prayer
Heavenly Father, we come to thank you for all the good things we enjoy in our lives. Especially we thank you that although you care for the whole universe you still listen to our prayers and answer them.

Thank you, Father, for Jesus your Son who showed by his example how important prayer is, and who taught us to pray. Help us to learn from him and to follow his example and teaching. *Say the Lord's Prayer together.*

Follow-up for the class-room

1   Read the story of the crippled man by the pool in Jerusalem: John 5.1-9. How does this compare with the story of the cripples in the Italian town in the time of St Francis?

2   Roman Catholics use rosaries to help them in their prayers. Find out what a rosary is and what it is used for.

3   The author of this short, simple prayer is unknown. Learn the prayer and talk in a group about its meaning.
God, grant me
   serenity to accept the things I cannot change,
   courage to change the things I can,
   and wisdom to know the difference.

Travelling on

The Assembly

Preparation
Obtain pictures of modern passenger aircraft, diesel locos, cars; and also of an old steam train, a horse and carriage, a sailing ship.

Introduction
Ask how people travelled about one hundred years ago. (They walked, rode on horseback, had carts and carriages drawn by horses, went on steam trains, and perhaps on steamers for sea voyages although sail had not gone completely. *As suggestions are made, display appropriate pictures.*) Up to the coming of steam in the 1830's most ordinary people travelled only a few miles from home. People from the next village were often referred to as strangers in the church registers. Even when trains had been running for forty years many ordinary people travelled very little. Perhaps they went for a train trip once or twice in a lifetime. In the 1880's there were very few motor cars and no aeroplanes. Roads for the most part were still very poor.

Now, most people travel a great deal. We think nothing of journeys of even thousands of miles by road, rail, air and sea. *(Display pictures of present-day travel.)*

What changes do you think there will be in the next hundred years? The greatest change will be that space travel for ordinary people may have arrived. There might be colonies in space in a hundred years' time.

Long ago travelling was so difficult it was often said that a journey was very like life. On a journey all kinds of difficulties were met, just as in life we meet difficulties. Journeys had to be taken in stages because it took so long to go even fairly short distances; life has some definite stages, too. Can you say what they are? (Childhood, youth, adulthood, middle age, old age.) Journeys had to have a definite aim: so much effort could not be used for nothing. Life, too, for Christian people, has a definite aim: we

122

are journeying towards God. It may seem that modern journeys are so easy and comfortable that we can no longer compare them with the journey of life. But that is not always so.

Reading
Paul described in one of his letters some of the dangers of travel in his day as he went about the Roman empire to preach the gospel of Jesus.

I have been in three shipwrecks, and once I spent twenty-four hours in the water. In my travels I have been in danger from floods and from robbers, in danger from fellow-Jews and from Gentiles; there have been dangers in the cities, dangers in the wilds, dangers on the high seas, and dangers from false friends. There has been work and toil; often I have gone without sleep; I have been hungry and thirsty; I have often been without enough food, shelter or clothing.

(2 Corinthians 11.25b-27, GNB)

Hymns
The journey of life   (CP 45)
When explorers sailed the oceans   (SNS 16)

Story
Ask how many have been on a motorway journey. Invite them to tell of some of the differences between travelling on a motorway and travelling on an ordinary road. (There are restrictions about who may use a motorway. They are one-way systems: traffic in the opposite direction is quite separate. They are very wide; most now have three lanes. All this makes for very fast traffic flow.) There is a speed limit *(mention the current limit)* and police patrols try to make people keep to the limit. There is also a very elaborate system of signals and notices and signs. Police can flash warning signals to advise motorists to reduce speed when conditions are bad. Huge notices tell drivers of roads and places en route. These remarkable roads enable us to do journeys in a few hours which once would have taken all day.

Dave Thomas quite liked motorways. He was a salesman and since the spread of motorways he found he could complete his journeys much more quickly and so spend more time at home with his wife and two young children. Before, he often had to spend nights away from home in dreary hotels. He liked motorway driving, too, because he could listen to the radio and feel quite relaxed most of the time.

There were times though when he did not enjoy driving home along the M6. Usually this was in late autumn or winter when fogs could close in quickly. One day, late in November, was such a time. It was misty and very wet. Dave moved into the inside lane and slowed down from 70mph to about 60. The fog was thickening; visibility was about 150 yards (or metres). Then he saw the hazard lights flashing and a lighted 50mph sign. 'Must be getting worse ahead,' he thought. He slowed to 50mph. A lorry behind began flashing its headlights. Dave tried to ignore it. The lorry pulled out and accelerated away, horn blasting the chill air, covering Dave's windscreen with a cascade of filthy spray.

The fog closed in. Dave began to feel quite worried. Visibility was down to less than 100 yards (or metres) now. But he was being passed by a constant stream of traffic. Much of it consisted of heavy lorries with cars dodging in and out of the fast lane. There was a lot of headlight flashing. It was difficult to keep the windscreen clear, because of the muddy spray outside and the steamy atmosphere inside. Hazard lights now showed 30mph maximum. But a kind of madness seemed to have overtaken many drivers that night. Cars and lorries flashed past Dave at speeds close to 70mph. Dave found that, with the closing darkness, the thickening fog, the mud and rain and dazzle, even 30mph seemed fast. He thought, 'I must get off this motorway at the next junction, even if it makes me rather late.'

He began to look for signs to turn off ahead. Then he saw flashing lights strung out across the motorway, and a cluster of red lights. Vehicles were being directed onto the hard shoulder. As Dave slowed right down and pulled over he wound down his window and called out to a policeman standing beside his Range Rover, 'What's wrong?'

'Pile-up ahead!' replied the policeman. 'Heaven knows how many. They've just piled into each other. Must be twenty or thirty involved.'

'Can I help?' asked Dave. And the policeman nodded, directing him to drive into the area beyond the flashing lights. Dave got out and ran ahead to do what he could to help. It was sheer chaos. Cars were strewn across the motorway. One was upside down. Another was trapped under a lorry. Glass and torn metal were everywhere. Dave worked for what seemed like hours, comforting those trapped in their vehicles, or wandering round in a dazed condition. It was with enormous relief that he saw the rescue services arrive. Firemen came with cutting apparatus. Ambulancemen began to carry the injured to the waiting ambulances. Doctors and nurses were busy everywhere as well as police. They were grateful for an extra pair of helping hands.

It was hours before Dave could proceed on his journey home. That was one journey he would never forget as long as he lived.

Comment
That modern story illustrates that travelling even nowadays can be difficult and dangerous. Perhaps it helps us understand how journeys can be said to be like the journey of life.

Hymns
He who would valiant be
Life is like a journey in a strange and foreign land   (SNS 67)
One more step along the world I go   (CP 47)

Prayer
Lord, we know that there will be difficulties to face as we go on life's journey. Help us to meet them with courage. Especially we pray that we may be amongst those who try to help others in their difficulties and so find our own troubles lighter.

Follow-up for the class-room

1   Recall the story and discuss the following questions. How does the story illustrate different experiences in life? (There are pleasant, easy times; there are times of stress and difficulty and crisis.) How does the story show us the different sorts of people we may meet in life? (There are sensible, considerate people. There are thoughtless, selfish people who involve others in their disasters. There are helpful people who tackle the mess and get things going again.) What sort of people are group members going to be? (Helpers or destroyers? Those who care or those who care only for themselves?)

2   Modern travellers have a Highway Code to help them travel safely. If we think of life as a journey we can think of the Bible as a book which helps us travel through life. Read Mark 12.28-31. Here Jesus sums up much of the teaching of the Old Testament. Write out the verses and learn Jesus' words from verses 29-31.

3   The nave of the church is the part where the congregation sits during services. Look up this word in a dictionary; how does it suggest that life is like a journey? In the journey of life we are travelling together. In the church are things which help us on the way. Arrange a visit to a local church and drawn the font, the lectern, the pulpit and the altar or communion table. Label the drawings and say what each item is used for.

4   The Bible tells about many journeys. One of the most famous is the journey from Egypt into the desert of Sinai made by the Israelites under Moses. There were many difficulties. Read Exodus 17. The Israelites wandered for forty years in the desert; what would this have taught them and how would it have helped them when they finally settled in Canaan?

Abbreviations and acknowledgements

The following abbreviations have been used in this book:

CP   Come and Praise
GNB   Good News Bible
NEB   New English Bible
SNS   Sing New Songs

The authors and publishers are grateful for permission to quote from the following:

Good News Bible, © American Bible Society 1976 (Bible Societies/Collins);
New English Bible, Second edition © 1970 (Oxford and Cambridge University Presses);
Words to Share (NCEC), 'The New Year' by Jack and Edna Young;
Good Morning, God (NCEC), 'Differences' by Lilian Cox;
Christmas Candles (NCEC), 'Saturday before Christmas' by Lilian Cox.

Bible readings

The following readings have been included in this book: